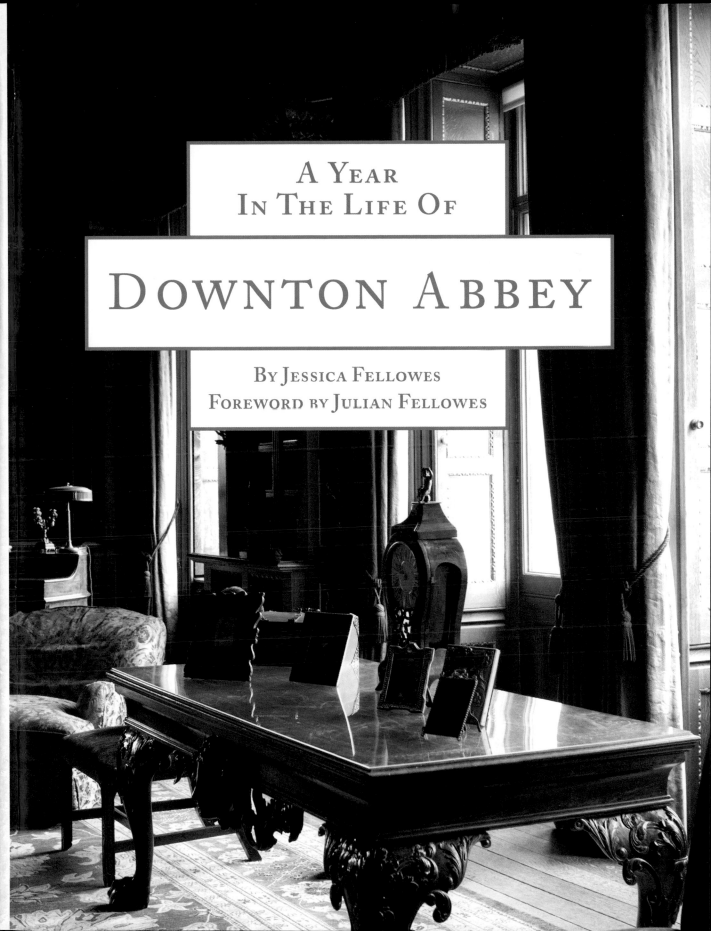

A Year
In The Life Of

Downton Abbey

By Jessica Fellowes
Foreword by Julian Fellowes

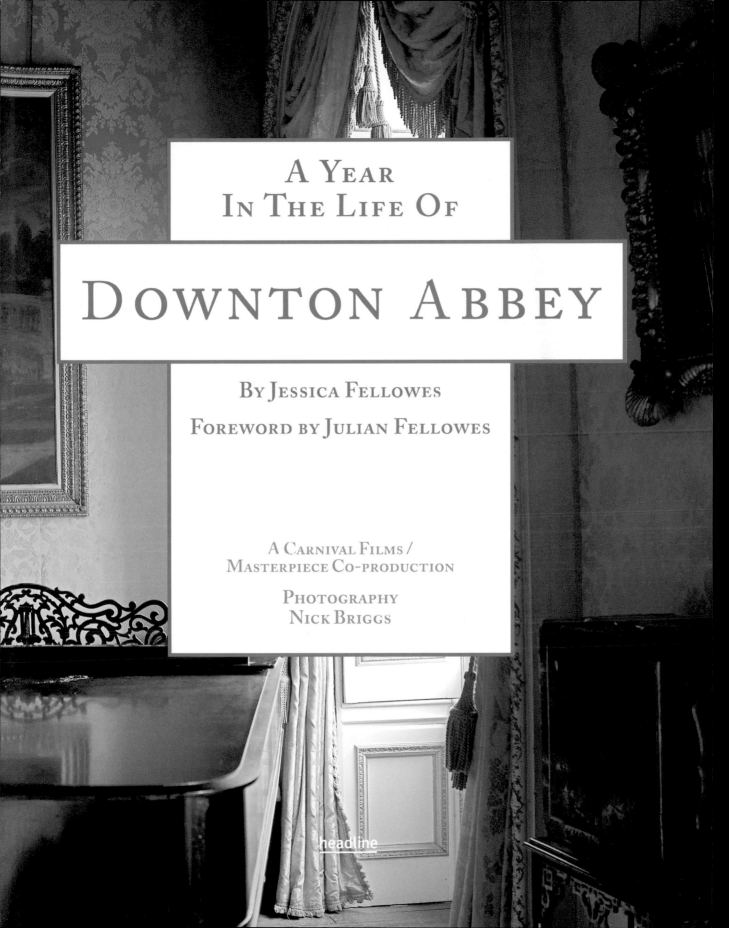

A Year
In The Life Of

Downton Abbey

By Jessica Fellowes

Foreword by Julian Fellowes

A Carnival Films /
Masterpiece Co-production

Photography
Nick Briggs

headline

CONTENTS

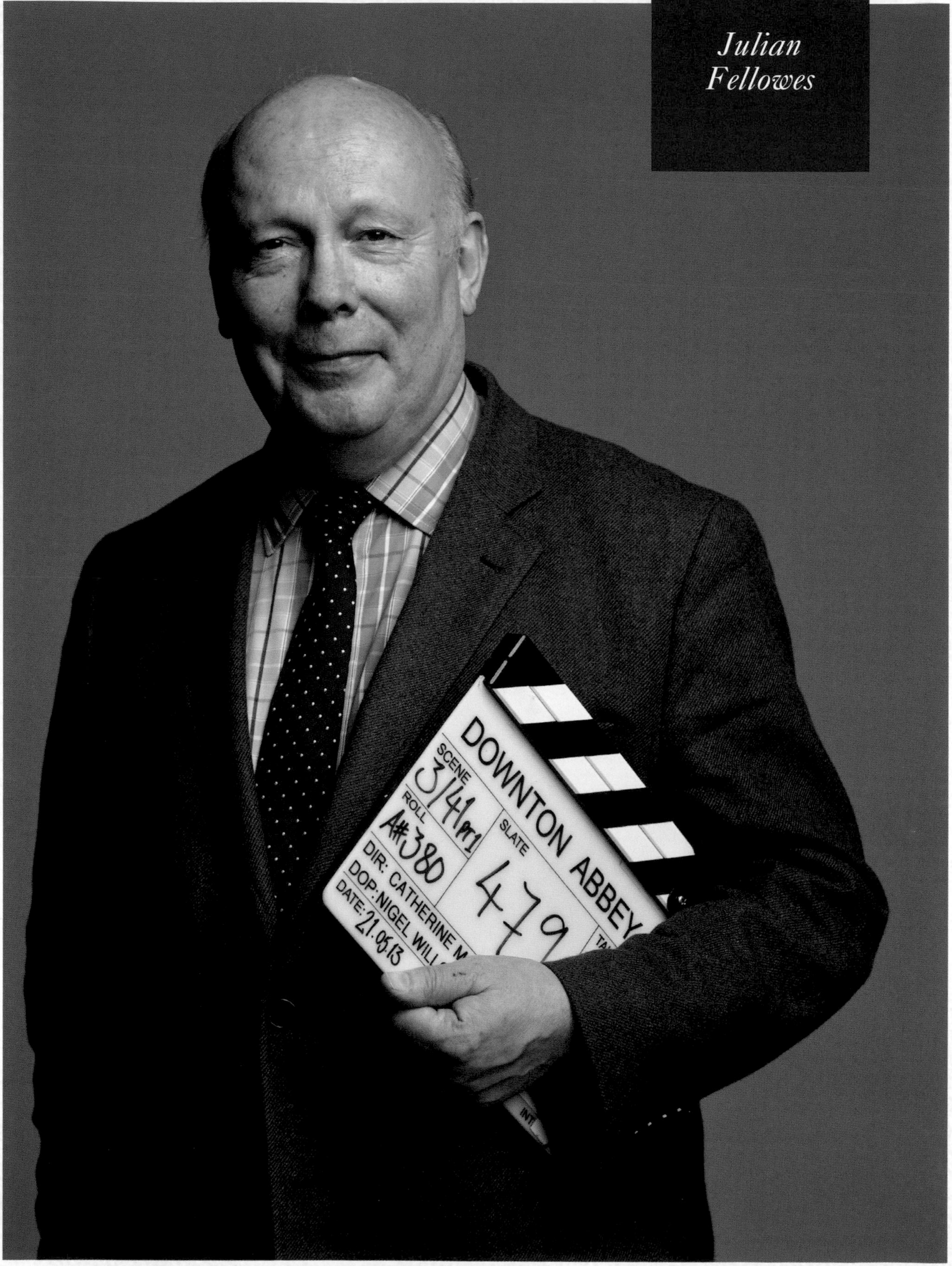

Julian Fellowes

FOREWORD

It seems strange to think that we have completed the fifth series of *Downton Abbey*, that we have taken these people through twelve years of change, through a war from which they emerged into a very different world, through all the emotional hiccoughs that are part of the human journey, much of which will be examined in this, the fourth book of the show. I like the idea of recording the Downton year. It seems a good device to me, since there is no question that life for the people who lived in these houses, their activities, their clothes, the very food they ate, was entirely dominated by the rhythm of the changing seasons. That has almost gone now. Central heating, imported produce, the abolition of formality, have collaborated to achieve a kind of twelve-month sameness. You see summer dresses at a New Year's Eve party and most of us have lost all connection with when vegetables and fruit are ripe for eating, because when they are not, the gap is supplied from abroad.

But like so many other aspects of life that we have shown, as we trace the trials and tribulations of the Crawley family and their dependants, this was different until very recently. In my own childhood and early teenage years, we lived in a house in Sussex, and my mother would arrive from London, usually on Friday morning (she would drive down after she had seen my father carried away to his male world), and the gardener would have laid out a selection of vegetables that were ready. The system had its drawbacks. You would eat broccoli or cabbage or Brussels sprouts, each in their own true season, until they were coming out of your ears, but yet, even then, when we thought nothing of such things, there was a kind of comforting rightness to it that artichokes from the Sudan or blueberries from Chad cannot quite match.

I remember very well the day things changed. I must have been about sixteen. My father finally sat down and worked out that every potato was costing him about twenty times more than if it were bought in a shop and he announced at dinner that the kitchen garden was to go. My mother was rather sad and managed to save the peach wall and some strawberry beds under netting, but before long the rest was history. They dug a rather inefficient (and freezing) swimming pool in one corner of the walled garden, and the rest supplied us with a badminton court and a place where all the Christmas trees from then on were planted. This was before the modern habit of removing their roots. I liked the Christmas grove, where the trees had grown quite big before the house was sold a quarter of a century later, and I didn't mind the court, or even the deficient pool, although I seldom swam, but there was something that had gone from our annual round and I suppose that, like so much else in the self-consciously changing world of the 1960s, it was because we were less connected to the soil than we had been.

As Jessica shows in this book, sports were a huge determinant of the annual round among the Crawleys and their kind, more perhaps before the war than ever again. There were many men, my own grandfather included, who didn't seem to do anything but sport, certainly not with any real interest. Shooting began in August, with grouse in the north, then came partridges, followed by pheasant, which ended, then as now, on 1 February (not, as I have seen printed many times, on 31 January). Shooting parties suited the constrictions of the late Victorians as they offered an opportunity for people to meet and flirt and generally get to know each other when they were not related, but at the same time, shooting seemed to give a purpose to a house party to mask the real reason, romantic or ambitious, for the introductions. Other sports, like fishing and sailing, tended to draw in the enthusiasts, but they did not have the wide appeal of shooting, which more or less every man of a certain type was expected to be able to do whether or not he was particularly good at it. Even hunting was restricted to a smaller group, although, after shooting, it was definitely the most social sport. Years later Evelyn Waugh, who was a keen follower of hounds for many years, admitted that his reasons for supporting the hunt were completely social. Certainly the hunting set in most counties could never have been accused of not smiling on flirtations of all sorts.

Cricket had a role in a country-house summer. More than any other sport practised by the occupants of the great houses, it had the potential to draw the different elements of the community into a single challenge, and there were many examples of the House playing the Village, or the Estate Workers playing the House, and so on. Cricket is hard to explain to those who are not keen, and I am not a sportsman in any case, but even I can remember the matches of village cricket in my youth with nostalgic affection. There is something about the sound of that soft rather lazy ripple of applause, as a community sprawls around a local game, making daisy chains and eyeing the tea tent, that is more evocative of the English summer than almost anything.

Sometimes people took the opportunity, after shooting and hunting were done, for travel in warmer climes, but by the spring the London Season was really under way, its first official date the Summer Exhibition at the Royal Academy. It would continue, at a hectic pace, until the end of June, and there would follow sojourns in the country, when cricket would have its moment, but it wasn't long before it was time to go north and start killing things again.

I think clothes were the final defining element of the fashionable year. Now, people cheerfully wear much the same things from January to December without a lot of variation. Lighter suits for men when the weather gets warm, a few more

'We have taken these people through twelve years of change'

floaty dresses for women when the sun is really beating down, although, as I have said, you will still see them when the leaves are off the trees. But then, there were four wardrobes for a well-dressed woman, spring, summer, autumn and winter and this never varied. This was the heyday of the great fashion houses. They had been going since Charles Frederick Worth opened his own shop, Maison Worth, in 1858, conquering the Second Empire in the process, but I think it was between the wars and for a decade or so after that the rule − or tyranny − of the fashion leaders held mightiest sway. In the series, we mention Patou and Lucile and Molyneux and various others, and all these designers had their followings. Lucile was glamorous but safe, Patou more daring, Molyneux definitively chic, and so on. Every woman, even those far from the catchment of these great stars, would follow their lead and assemble different wardrobes for the seasons. Even my own mother, who certainly had no money − or not what she would have called 'real money' − would go on four modest buying sprees a year, usually blaming the expenditure on the sartorial demands of our school's 'Summer Exhibition', viz. the headmaster's dinner, the garden party at our prep school, High Mass, etc., when my father questioned her. But she continued the practice after the last of us had left. Today, some women do much the same of course and good luck to them, but for most of the population, the sub-division of a wardrobe into seasons seems to have subsided or vanished altogether.

And so the years ran on, through the twenties with the strange Janus-like quality of that era, facing back into the nineteenth century as well as ushering in so many of the inventions that would define the modern world; followed by the thirties, with the decade's sharp contrasts of carefree luxury and terrifying want, as the privileged were released from so many of the strictures and rules that had governed their parents' choices, while the less fortunate were fighting their way through the collapse of the economy. Until finally Britain reached the war, six years of fighting that would wash away any lingering doubt that the old world had vanished like the snows of yesteryear. There was a brief chimera to be gone through in the 1950s when the government wanted to put the returning soldiers back to work and women were encouraged, in campaign after campaign, to return to their pre-war, even Edwardian, role; when Dior and the other houses would revive the crinoline, when white tie came back for men, but these times were an illusion. No government on earth was able to persuade men, let alone women, that nothing had changed, and their Canute-like attempts to stem the tide came to an abrupt end in the sixties, when the Beatles and the Rolling Stones blew such notions out of the water forever, leaving us all as citizens of the New Age.

Julian Fellowes
July 2014

SERIES 5 CAST LIST

Matt Barber
ATTICUS ALDRIDGE

Samantha Bond
LADY ROSAMUND PAINSWICK

Hugh Bonneville
THE EARL OF GRANTHAM (ROBERT)

Laura Carmichael
LADY EDITH CRAWLEY

Jim Carter
CHARLES CARSON

Raquel Cassidy
PHYLLIS BAXTER

Brendan Coyle
JOHN BATES

Tom Cullen
TONY GILLINGHAM

Michelle Dockery
LADY MARY CRAWLEY

Penny Downie
LADY SINDERBY

Kevin Doyle
JOSEPH MOLESLEY

Peter Egan
THE MARQUESS OF FLINTSHIRE
(SHRIMPIE)

James Faulkner
LORD SINDERBY

Joanne Froggatt
ANNA BATES

Richard E. Grant
SIMON BRICKER

Lily James
LADY ROSE MACCLARE

Robert James-Collier
THOMAS BARROW

Sue Johnston
DENKER

Jane Lapotaire
PRINCESS IRINA

Allen Leech
TOM BRANSON

Daisy Lewis
SARAH BUNTING

Phyllis Logan
ELSIE HUGHES

Emma Lowndes
MRS DREWE

Elizabeth McGovern
THE COUNTESS OF GRANTHAM (CORA)

Sophie McShera
DAISY MASON

Phoebe Nicholls
SUSAN, THE MARCHIONESS
OF FLINTSHIRE

Lesley Nicol
BERYL PATMORE

Julian Ovenden
CHARLES BLAKE

Douglas Reith
LORD MERTON

David Robb
DR CLARKSON

Andrew Scarborough
TIM DREWE

Rade Sherbedgia
PRINCE KURAGIN

Maggie Smith
THE DOWAGER COUNTESS
OF GRANTHAM (VIOLET)

Ed Speleers
JIMMY KENT

Catherine Steadman
MABEL LANE FOX

Jeremy Swift
MR SPRATT

Harriet Walter
LADY SHACKLETON

Penelope Wilton
ISOBEL CRAWLEY

JANUARY
The Year Ahead

Mr Carson

JANUARY

A thin white line on the horizon signals the dawn of a new year at Downton Abbey. The house sits atop its cold hill, the valley falling below, still shrouded in darkness, as the servants start to shuffle around slowly, waking in the icy air of their attic bedrooms.

Lady Mary stirs below her blankets; she shan't wake till a maid has lit the fire to warm the bedroom. Besides, there would have been a celebratory dinner the night before, a glass or two of Champagne at midnight before the cheers for 1924 sent her up the stairs. We have faith that the year ahead brings her new feelings of hope and vigour – in series four, we watched her allow herself to start living a life that looks forward after the death of her beloved Matthew. Lord and Lady Grantham slumber too, together in their bed, perhaps forestalling the moment when they open their eyes to a world that has been changing at a pace that often leaves them feeling bewildered rather than excited. Lady Edith lies awake in the dark – troubled thoughts are never far away, but she can only hope this year is better than the last, with her daughter no longer overseas and safely looked after only a short walk away. Tom Branson snores lightly; I like to imagine he's the kind of father to creep up the stairs to the nursery, to kiss his daughter Sybbie good morning before he goes down to breakfast. Nanny wouldn't always approve of the disruption to the children's routine, but surely Tom remembers how his mother was in the cottage he grew up in, in Ireland, and would not be able to resist. The day will be an easy one for the family, a few guests to entertain before the morrow's shoot, but no business to attend to or errands to run. There will be a long lunch, a walk in the afternoon, another dinner in the evening.

For the servants, of course, their day is quite different, in that it is exactly the same as almost every other day when it comes to their duties and routine. They will have had a small New Year's Eve celebration of their own in the servants' hall, one that would have livened up considerably once Carson and Mrs Hughes had gone to bed shortly after midnight struck. A few of them will wake regretting the last glass of beer they drank. But there's no shirking; the house must be got ready, shutters opened and fires made, rugs swept and the table laid. Two breakfasts need to be cooked, two luncheons must be prepared (for the family and for the servants),

the menu for the family's dinner written out. Carson is up and at the head of the table below stairs as smartly on time as he is every single other day of the year.

For the fifth series, we have returned to Downton Abbey in 1924. It may be only twelve years since we first stepped through the vast wooden door of the castle and met the cast of characters we are now so familiar with, but the changes have been so great, it is as if a century has passed. Change has been the theme of *Downton Abbey* since it began, reflecting the extraordinary developments in science and society that happened in the real world during the same period. But it is only now, as we head into the middle of the 1920s, that the full effects of those changes are being absorbed into our characters' daily lives.

The differences between 1912 and 1924 are marked: motorcars are a frequent sight on the roads; a passenger may travel to Paris by aeroplane as easily as by ferry; women have seats in the House of Commons; the hems of women's dresses are several inches shorter and the corset has almost been consigned to history. More tragically, a generation of young men has been killed in a brutal war.

By contrast, what we witness at Downton Abbey is a world that still prefers to move slowly. The drama comes as we watch our friends and see how they each react in their own ways to these modern intrusions. Some are sympathetic, some fight against them, others actively encourage them along.

'At Skelton Park, they're down to a butler, a cook, two maids and a cleaning woman who comes in from the village. And that's their lot.'

MRS HUGHES

CARSON: *'It puts us back in agreement, Mrs Hughes. I'm not comfortable when you and I are not in agreement.'*

MRS HUGHES: *'You're very flattering. When you talk like that, you make me want to check in the looking glass to see that my hair's tidy.'*

CARSON: *'Get away with you.'*

The gatekeeper to Downton Abbey is Mr Carson – our fierce defender of the old way of life. The butler of the house, he holds absolute superiority below stairs – and occasionally, it seems, above stairs too. Carson knows the glory days are behind him – the so-called long Edwardian summer before the war, when he enjoyed a full retinue of servants at his command, liveried and polished, always at the ready to serve the nobility in the dining room. Now he must scrape along with Thomas as under-butler and Jimmy and Molesley for footmen; he's even endured a maid serving in the dining room. Most unsettlingly of all, rather than a family of pure blue blood, the former chauffeur, Tom Branson, now sits at the dinner table. Snob though he is, we must try to be sympathetic. If Carson minds so terribly about whether or not the correct pudding glasses have been put out, it is because he feels that unless he does so, the whole world may as well have gone to rack and ruin and his entire life and career will be completely without meaning. Of course, every house did things differently, but the code by which Carson lives is not simply a set of rules to manage the Downton household – it underpins his very existence.

Mrs Hughes, as housekeeper, is Carson's ally below stairs and together they rule the servants, managing not only their daily tasks, but giving them guidance in their personal lives. In many respects, Carson and Mrs Hughes are the mirror reflection of their master and mistress, Lord and Lady Grantham, as the parents of the servant family. Mrs Hughes is different to Carson in one important respect, however – while she enjoys her job, with the dignity and responsibility that it brings, she is not in thrall to her employers. Mrs Hughes has a career and, although it does not seem that she has much time away from it, there is a definite sense that she has, at the very least, a life of her own, if only for an hour or two at a time. It means that she is able to regard the changes in the world with a sympathetic eye – not any moral lapses, mind, but when it comes to relieving the work of the maids with an electrical gadget or two, she is more than happy to try new things.

The last time we saw Carson and Mrs Hughes they were walking hand in hand together into the sea. Could this be the beginning of a romance? If it is, it would not be altogether surprising, as many butlers went into retirement to open a seaside hotel with their former housekeepers or housemaids. Of course, we hope that this would be more than a pragmatic arrangement between our two much-loved characters, but we shall have to wait and see.

*All documents seen on the show have been made
by the art department, using authentic paper and ink.*

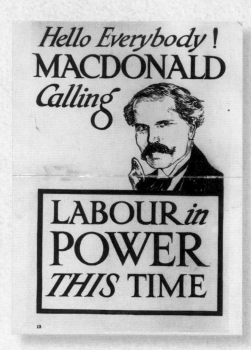

Hello Everybody! MACDONALD Calling

LABOUR in POWER THIS TIME

JIMMY: *'Well, I think it's fantastic. When did we last have a prime minister who understood the working class? Never. That's when.'*

CARSON: *'It's a qualification that is meaningless in terms of Government.'*

Beyond the vast, rolling grounds of Downton Abbey the political landscape is changing – so drastically that the effects are felt even in the depths of this great house. In January 1924, Stanley Baldwin's Conservative government lost a vote of no confidence and Ramsay MacDonald became Britain's first Labour prime minister. It was a minority government and MacDonald was, in fact, to lose the general election the following year to his old rival, Baldwin. But even so, to have a Labour government in power at all signified a huge shift in traditional British politics, where the aristocracy had ruled the country practically since a government had formed. While the socialist movement had been gathering pace since the middle of the previous century, the 1924 election proved that the winds had changed for good. The working classes were at last able to believe that it was possible for them to have a say in how their country was run (many had only been able to vote for the first time when suffrage was extended in 1919); aristocrats could no longer sit comfortably in the belief that they had a divine right to rule. Quite the opposite. It wouldn't be going too far to say that the upper classes believed that they were under attack – certainly, this is how Robert and Violet feel.

In short, the idea that everyone knew their place in society and was happy to adhere to it had finally broken down completely. For people like Robert, Violet and Carson, the only result could be chaos. But for others, it meant hope.

However, while ideas may be changing, the practical daily life of Downton Abbey is out of step with the pace. That is, so long as Carson has anything to do with it. As the year begins, he will be keen to ensure that those matters over which he has jurisdiction will run along the same well-oiled lines he has always presided over. 'He is struggling to keep everything the same,' says Jim Carter, of his character. 'He believes he is the guardian of the standards, and while he is ultimately pragmatic, the sands are shifting beneath his feet.'

MRS HUGHES
*'I think it's exciting.
We're catching up, Mr
Carson. Whether you
like it or not, Downton
is catching up with the
times we live in.'*

CARSON
*'That is exactly what
I am afraid of.'*

So it is that, as the day begins, Carson will continue to keep his place at the head of the table in the servants' hall, Mrs Hughes on his right, as Daisy serves the hot toast for their breakfast. Carson's scrambled eggs are served to him by the hall boy, a youngster of fourteen or fifteen years old, in training to be a footman. The other servants – Bates, Anna, Baxter, Mr Barrow (for he must be addressed as such, now he is under-butler), Molesley and the other housemaids – are ranged around the table in strict hierarchical order, as was ever thus. The servants are fewer and the household budget is smaller in this post-war world, but Carson still does his best to maintain a pre-war air.

Despite his troubles, Carson is supported in his determination to stick to the old ways by his working relationship with Lord Grantham. For a master and his butler to be together for years was not uncommon and for many men, their butler was the one ally in whom they could confide most openly about their worries when it came to matters of the family. Husbands who did not wish to worry their wives about household budgets always turned to their butlers first. They may also have simply found it reassuring that there was someone else in charge in the house – one who knew exactly how to tend the excellent management of the wine cellar or ensure the fires were lit and the silver perfectly polished when there were guests to impress. Julian Fellowes remembers his wife's ninety-year-old aunt sadly recalling the year her father's butler died: 'They had been together a long time ... he was very quiet that summer.'

Spratt

Not that our friends at Downton Abbey are always perfect. The Dowager Countess, Violet, a stalwart believer in the old ways, is not such a friend of her own butler – although, perhaps, the women rarely were, preferring the confidences of their lady's maids.

But quite apart from the fact that it was nicer at home if you liked the people you lived with, whether as employer or employee, there was also the matter of pride at stake. Lord and Lady Grantham need to remain at the top of the social ladder by ensuring any noble or important guests that come to stay are impressed by the grandeur and comfort in which they live.

ISOBEL: *'It seems rather unlikely. To think of Spratt with a private life.'*

VIOLET: *'Yes, unlikely and extremely inconvenient.'*

ISOBEL: *'But you can't begrudge him that, surely. Servants are human beings, too.'*

VIOLET: *'Yes. But preferably only on their days off.'*

> *'There'll come a time when a household is lucky to boast any footmen.'*
>
> MRS HUGHES

For Carson and Mrs Hughes, this means putting on a good show for these guests, demonstrating their high professional standards. Part of their job is to instil this motivation in the younger servants. Those who do well will enjoy promotion, either at Downton Abbey or elsewhere. There existed an efficient underground servants' network which passed along news of vacancies as well as gossip about any employers who treated their servants badly. The real challenge that faces our two most experienced and senior servants at Downton Abbey is that the younger generation no longer feel the same way about service as they did when starting out. It is neither the respected nor safe career it was before the war. While Carson and Mrs Hughes see their positions in an earl's household as prestigious, the pinnacle of a successful career and most likely a welcome escape from alternative lives as a music-hall act or farmer's wife, the younger servants are weighing up new, sometimes much more attractive options.

After the war, those who lived in the rural areas of the country no longer had to choose solely between farming or service for a career. Train travel meant that going further afield for work was not the daunting separation from one's family that it once had been. New technology opened up exciting possibilities and those who were clever could aim to be electricians (revered as 'men of science') or chauffeurs. Even the women could leave and find jobs as telephonists or secretaries. Work in factories or shops, while not exactly new or better paid, was, thanks again to trains and motorcars, not quite as out of reach as it had been, with the plus that it offered much shorter working hours. These opportunities appealed to men who had fought in the war and had seen another way of life. It suited many of the big houses too, which had less money, thanks to the post-war high taxes, and had managed to survive without their usual retinue of servants when everyone was away fighting – they were less inclined to hire them all back again.

At Downton Abbey, some of these changes are being felt. There are rumblings from the likes of Thomas (though he's the type that will always find something to complain about) and Jimmy that there must be more to life than being a servant, and even mild-mannered Alfred has gone to London to work at the Ritz, flying in the face of his family's – and Carson's – expectations for him. But, for the most part, even in what he considers to be reduced circumstances, Carson puts his best face on it and sticks to the routine.

Mrs Hughes

Mrs Patmore

'The way things are going, life will be lived in much closer quarters in the future. My grandparents lived in vast rooms, surrounded by staff. If they disagreed they'd hardly have known it. But it won't be like that for us. I must be sure I'm right to want this man, as my friend, my lover, my husband.'

MARY

Mrs Hughes's housemaids will be up at 5.30 a.m. daily in order to get the house ready before the family comes down. Once Robert, Tom and Edith are down for breakfast, the maids move swiftly upstairs to make their beds and clean their bedrooms, before doing the same for Cora and Mary once they are up and dressed – as married women, they enjoy breakfast in bed. During the day, the maids are never seen in the public rooms by the family, but will do the remainder of their work below stairs or out of sight. The servants' quarters also have to be kept clean. Occasionally the maids may help out at mealtimes, carrying dishes between the kitchen and the dining room.

Carson, meanwhile, will be fussing Mr Barrow and the footmen to lay the table for breakfast before they have their own. As senior servants, they are served by hall boys and kitchen maids. (Mrs Patmore's kitchen assistants have, of course, also been up since dawn to begin their long cooking day.) Breakfast over, there will be various tasks, from polishing silver to serving coffee in the library or lighting the fires. Generally the footmen were thought to have the easiest jobs of the house, having been hired for their good looks and splendour in livery, all the better for impressing guests. The very best footmen were not only six foot tall, but exactly the same height as each other, which looked most impressive when they were standing either side of the front door.

With fewer guests arriving with their own valet or lady's maid these days, Carson and Mrs Hughes have to allocate a member of their own staff to do the job instead. Usually, this would fall to Mr Barrow and Anna. But there's been more reference to 'Madge' lately, the housemaid that dresses Edith, so she may be put to use for a low-ranking guest. After that, there are wine cellars to be managed, larder stocks to be assessed, household budgets to be monitored, spare bedrooms to be made up. Carson will liaise with the estate managers to make sure there are enough logs for the fireplaces; Mrs Hughes will talk to the gardener if a vase of flowers is beginning to lose its bloom. And at any time, anyone from the family may call upon them with a sharp ring on the bell, summoning a servant from whatever it is they may be doing, in order to attend to their needs – however trivial they may be.

One of the most compelling aspects of these large houses, with so many servants hurrying about, is the lack of privacy. For example, servants did not always knock on the door before entering a room, either because they knew they were expected or because they were in and out so often it would have slowed things down too much to do so. Married couples conducted their relationships almost entirely in a public space and some would argue that this kept them going for longer than they might have done had they only had each other to look at and talk to.

Jimmy

KEDGEREE

*One of Mrs Patmore's great standbys, this breakfast or supper dish dates
back to the days of the British Raj and has stood the test of time.
An excellent way to start the day – and the New Year.*

SERVES 4–6

500g smoked haddock fillet
1 tablespoon sunflower oil
50g butter
1 large onion, finely chopped
1 tablespoon curry powder
    or paste
200g basmati rice, rinsed
    and drained
a large handful of parsley leaves,
    chopped
a handful of raisins (optional)
salt and pepper
4 hard-boiled eggs
lemon wedges, to serve

Place the haddock in a medium saucepan, pour boiling water over
to cover it and poach for up to 10 minutes or until the fish is barely
cooked. Do not allow the water to re-boil. Remove the fish from the
water with a slotted spoon and set aside on a plate to cool. Keep the
cooking water in the pan.

Heat the sunflower oil and half the butter in a large saucepan.
Add the onion and cook over a low heat until softened – about
10 minutes. Stir in the curry powder and cook for another couple
of minutes. Add the rice to the pan and stir well. When the rice
is slightly translucent, pour in 600ml of the haddock cooking water
and bring to the boil. Simmer gently for about 15 minutes, stirring
occasionally, until all the liquid has been absorbed and the rice is
tender. Add a little more water if necessary. Take the pan off the heat.

Flake the haddock and add to the rice, along with the parsley, raisins
(if using), the remaining butter and a good grinding of salt and
pepper. Stir the mixture gently to combine and transfer to a serving
dish. Cut the hard-boiled eggs into quarters, scatter over the top
and serve immediately with lemon wedges on the side.

SEVILLE ORANGE MARMALADE

Seville oranges are in season for a short time in the weeks after Christmas and have been prized in England since the seventeenth century – particularly to make this delicious, bitter-tasting marmalade.

MAKES ABOUT 4.5KG (10 MEDIUM JARS)

1.5kg Seville oranges
2 lemons
3.5 litres water
2.5kg granulated sugar

Wash, rinse and dry the jars. Place a couple of saucers in the fridge.

Wash the oranges and lemons and cut in half. Squeeze out the juice and pips from the fruit. As you work, pour the juice into a jug and place the pips and any pith and membranes that cling to the squeezer into a bowl. Scoop out any pith that remains in the squeezed halves and add this to the bowl also.

Slice the fruit peel thinly (or thickly, depending on preference), and place in a large preserving pan. Add the reserved fruit juice and the water.

Place the collected pith and pips on a square of muslin and tie into a little bag using a length of string. Tie the string on to the handle of the pan so that the bag is submerged in the liquid. Bring to the boil and then simmer gently for about 2 hours, until the peel is really soft and the liquid reduced by about half.

At this point, pull out the muslin bag and squeeze it with two small plates to extract as much pectin as possible into the pan, then discard the bag. Add the sugar and stir until it has dissolved. Clip a sugar thermometer to the side of the pan and boil rapidly until setting point is reached (105°C/221°F) – about 15–20 minutes.

To test for a set, place a teaspoon of the mixture on to a cold saucer and put back in the fridge. Remove the pan from the heat while you do this. After a few minutes, push the mixture with your little finger – if it wrinkles, it is set. If not, continue to boil the marmalade and test again at 5–10 minute intervals. Once a set has been achieved, turn off the heat and leave to stand for about 15 minutes before potting. While it's cooling, scrape off any scum that has formed on the surface with a metal spoon and discard.

During this resting time, heat the prepared jars in a moderate oven for 5 minutes to sterilise them.

Using a funnel or ladle, pour the hot marmalade into the warm jars, cover immediately with waxed discs, then with dampened cellophane discs and secure with elastic bands. Store in a cool, dark place and use within 1 year.

Back in real life, Donal Woods, production designer, is perhaps the show's equivalent to Carson – kind and fair, but quietly authoritative. Despite the fact that Donal is responsible for numerous sets and locations, which must be designed from scratch, built, maintained, used, packed and stored, he makes it all seem as easy as putting up a Wendy house in the garden. There's something rather reassuring in the way that much of Downton's production proceeds in this enviably Downtonian manner. All of the most senior production crew exude calm on set. Perhaps it's because they know they have a very skilled crew to do the work, but perhaps the stately airs have rubbed off on them, in the best possible way. Doubtless, they would tell you that it isn't like that at all – much as Downton Abbey likes to appear calm, just below the surface the action is as frantic as a swan's paddling feet.

Filming a series takes around six months, beginning mid to late February and finishing in the middle of August, with one week off in May. About two or three weeks before shooting starts, cast and crew gather for the read-through of the first five episodes. Held in an anonymous, large, slightly chilly room somewhere in Ealing, there is always palpable excitement as everyone reunites, several months after they have wrapped the last series, but with the good news of climbing ratings, awards won, foreign territories achieved and critical acclaim garnered since it went on air still ringing in their ears. At the first ever reading, hardly anybody aside from the actors and a skeleton crew came along. At the fifth read-through, anyone, it seems, who can lay claim to being there, is there – the room is crowded with actors, crew, PRs and ITV staff. Scripts are guarded and carefully registered with anyone who borrows a copy, even if only for the day – if you take one home, your name will be watermarked across every page (that way, if a script is found, they'll know who left it lying about). The actors arrange themselves around a square of trestle tables, polystyrene cups of coffee in hand and rarely looking anything like their characters, with the benefit of modern-day make-up and skinny jeans.

Having received their scripts only a few days before, the actors may not even have read through all their lines. As Allen Leech joked, particularly during the years set in the First World War, they may simply want to know their character is still alive: 'I'd quickly flick to the back pages and if I saw "Branson opens car door", there would be a sigh of relief.' The main purpose of the read-through is for the producers and directors to see how the script is working – 'It is a great opportunity to hear the script for the first time,' says Liz Trubridge – and for key crew to anticipate anything that may be needed by way of lighting, special effects, props and so on. The actors need only 'read through' the lines, but of course no professional can do anything other than say the lines in character, and so to listen to it is rather like hearing a version of *Downton Abbey* on the radio (and wouldn't *that* be lovely?). Indeed, when Allen Leech and Jessica Brown Findlay first read the scene of Sybil's death, there wasn't a dry eye in the house.

Elizabeth McGovern and Richard E. Grant on location at the National Gallery.

After the read-through, the actors and crew are soon caught up in the whirling dervish that is pre-production. Donal Woods' team will have been building the sets at Ealing Studios since mid-January; they take about a month to put up, having been stored since August in a huge warehouse in Oxford. Few adjustments are made year on year, because Downton is a place that changes at a snail's pace. Personal knick-knacks may alter a little and there are some new sets to be designed and built – Donal will have had sight of the first plots for the forthcoming series since December, in order to think about what will be needed, from guest sets and new locations to select or even build, to adjustments to Mary's bedroom. Other factors need to be taken into consideration too, as the shooting of scenes is not done strictly in order of their appearance in the scripts. 'When it comes to new sets, it's about getting the balance right between logistics and creativity,' says Donal. 'We can spend up to four days on creating a single scene – as when we saw Edith go to the newspaper office in London. But that was important because we saw women typing and smoking in an office, something we don't normally see at Downton. It was a good way of showing what working women were like at that time. Occasionally, we may go back to Julian and request that something is set somewhere slightly different in order to make the logistics easier but if it's not good for the show, we won't do it.' Donal says he most enjoys creating those sets that are unexpected on *Downton*, such as the London nightclubs or the workhouse: 'They're a little bit out of the obvious and change the pace. The sets can be very elaborate and are great fun to do.'

When the last nail has been banged into the set walls, the final button sewn on to a dress and hair perfectly coiffed, the actors will step on set to say their lines in front of camera. Carson and Mrs Hughes will have the house shipshape and Bristol fashion, ready to face the new year ahead and all the challenges it will inevitably bring them at Downton Abbey.

Michelle Dockery and Tom Cullen on location for series five.

GARETH NEAME
EXECUTIVE PRODUCER

When Gareth Neame and Julian Fellowes met for dinner in Chelsea a few years ago, it didn't at first look as if it was going to be a very productive meeting. First of all, the restaurant they had planned to go to was shut, so they tramped around until they found an unassuming Italian bistro. Initially, they had planned the meeting in order to say goodbye to a project that they had not been able to make fly. As they talked, Gareth said he thought that a television series based on the world Julian so beautifully explored in his screenplay *Gosford Park* would work brilliantly. 'I had long thought that the setting of an English country house during the Edwardian era would make a very suitable arena for an episodic television series, with its joy of repeated pleasure because your audience is able to connect with the characters on a weekly basis.'

Despite an animated conversation over supper, Julian later said something to the effect of lightning not striking twice in the same place (he had won an Oscar for his script, taking him from unknown writer and character actor to Hollywood hot property in what was a literal overnight sensation) and Gareth thought that might be it until he received an email from Julian, no more than a couple of pages long, describing his initial thoughts on all the major characters who would come to inhabit Downton. 'I had a strong sense that Julian had lived with these characters for many years, but was only now describing them on the page,' says Gareth. 'At once the world came alive for me.'

Lesley Nicol, Phyllis Logan and Sophie McShera discuss their next scene.

Cut to 2014 – the production is shooting its fifth series, and the show has been seen by more than 270 million viewers worldwide. It has won just about every TV award there is, from Emmys to Golden Globes, and is the most successful British-made television export ever. It is, safe to say, evident that lightning does indeed strike twice.

Each year the show gets bigger, garnering more fans in ever far-reaching places (Jim was astonished to be recognised when he was cycling in Cambodia). Does this put more pressure on Gareth? 'The biggest challenge with a show as beloved as *Downton* is that you've got to keep it up there – there can't be any drop-off in terms of quality,' he explains. 'That can be difficult, given the sheer weight of narrative we carry. We have to try to find fresh ways of doing things yet retain the elements people love. Familiarity is a huge part of the appeal and we do have a sense now of how the likes of Violet, Carson or Tom Branson are going to react to the circumstances we put them in. But it has to be kept airborne – we have to find the balance between the expected and the unexpected.'

The show itself isn't the only thing to get bigger – so are the actors' profiles: 'Everyone wants a piece of the cast and that can be a juggling act for our schedule. Fortunately, the advantage of an ensemble cast is that they're not all called every day for filming.'

Gareth's own *Downton* year begins as soon as shooting wraps in August; at that point, while everything is still fresh in their minds, he and Julian have several meetings to brainstorm the next series. Gareth has had a set of laminated photographs made up for each character – 'We'll hold one up and discuss their storyline,' he says. 'You'll have people accusing you of getting out the darts,' I say. 'In a way it is a bit like that,' laughs Gareth. 'Julian will say, for some characters, that he absolutely knows what he wants to do with them, while others are less clear so we'll brainstorm and develop ideas together. But that's how the storyline of Anna's assault and resulting impact on her marriage evolved.'

Of course, some storylines are forced when an actor decides to leave. Dan Stevens (Matthew Crawley), Jessica Brown Findlay (Lady Sybil) and Siobhan Finneran (O'Brien) left to pursue other acting opportunities. 'We had a lot of notice for Sybil's exit and as we had three daughters, we were OK to lose one and we knew that it could be a great piece of storytelling, which it was. Dan Stevens' exit was much harder – we didn't know until just a few episodes before the finale, plus we had already had one death that series. It had to be that way [for Matthew and Sybil] because a servant can be fired, but if we lose someone from the family the only possible exit is through death. We couldn't have Mary and Matthew estranged so soon after their marriage either. We had very few episodes in which to lay a footpath for his leaving, so [the car crash] was the only option,' explains Gareth.

From September to December as Julian writes the first drafts, Gareth will be involved in new actor deals, hiring directors, and the post-production of the previous series right through the autumn season as the finale does not air until Christmas. By Christmas, the first four episodes will have been written and shared with key production members, with two more arriving in January. There's a short working break at this point in the new year, when the awards season kicks off in America with the Emmys and the various Guild awards.

The crew's call-sheet.

The scripts will have been completed by June but filming begins at the end of February and runs through until August, during which time post-production (editing, music) is ongoing. Post-production and publicity continues after they have wrapped until they deliver their final episode in December. Throughout the year, there's a lot of international travel for Gareth and the cast: 'Although we make the show in the UK, it's as big, if not bigger, in the US and growing elsewhere, so we'll be going to China, Australia, New Zealand…' All the while, of course, Gareth is busy as managing director of Carnival Films, producing other TV dramas and developing new ideas.

'I genuinely love the show,' says Gareth, smiling. 'If I didn't make it, I'd be watching it.' But while Gareth has enjoyed a number of professional successes (*Spooks, State of Play* and *Whitechapel,* to name just a few), the phenomenon of *Downton Abbey* is unique. 'I hoped we'd do well, but the shock was the scale of success, not just in America but in European countries typically not much interested in British TV, such as France and Spain. Then there's China…!' Does he have a theory for the show's success? Gareth nods: 'It starts with being an expressly British and familiar genre – the aristocracy in the English country house – which we know from Agatha Christie, P. G. Wodehouse and Jane Austen. But where previously it's been literary or sedate or a little old-fashioned, what we've done is provide sharp, pacy, modern storytelling with multiple narratives. So firstly, it's familiar, and secondly, it's slightly unexpected. Thirdly, the characters are so well drawn and acted you can relate to them. I think also we show romance in a way that isn't seen much anymore – the will they/won't they element that audiences enjoy. There's comedy, there's the strong sense of family… We've lined up all these ducks in a row.'

Gareth made a deliberate decision to take the idea to ITV: 'We were trying to do something fresh, non literary and revive the genre of period drama. So I had an idea that the show needed to be where you wouldn't quite expect to find it. ITV is a mainstream entertainment channel and on Sunday nights – if we got it right – then three generations of a family watching *The X Factor* would stay with the channel at 9 p.m. and find *Downton.* Often one makes a plan and it doesn't entirely turn out as predicted. But in the case of which broadcaster to take the idea of *Downton* to, it worked precisely according to plan. I think perhaps, if this isn't too bold a claim, we've reinvented the genre for the twenty-first century.'

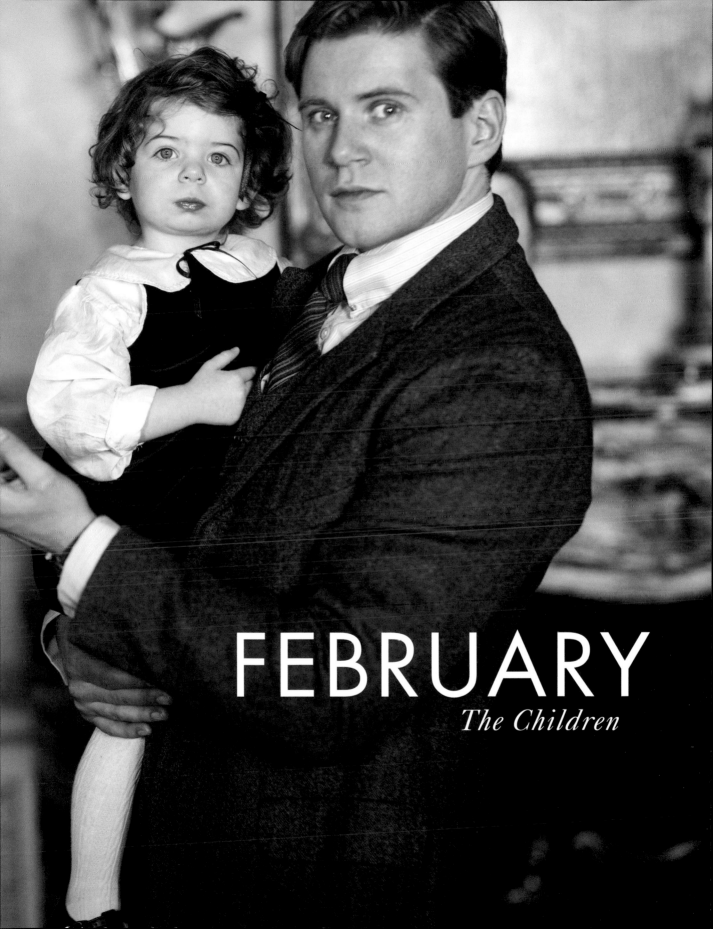

FEBRUARY

The Children

Master
George
Crawley

FEBRUARY

Go up the stairs at Downton Abbey, until you are out of sight and hearing from the drawing room and library, and you will hear the squeals and shouts of two small children, Master George and Miss Sybbie, as they chase each other down the hall.

ot since Mary, Edith and Sybil were little girls have tiny hands smudged the walls of the nursery and their happy, innocent noises are a delight to a house that is still reeling from the deaths of George's father and Sybbie's mother. The two young cousins are less than a year apart in age, but this shared bereavement – both lost a parent within hours of their birth – is sure to make them as close as twins.

George is currently the heir apparent to the earldom; his mother, Mary, is the owner of what was Matthew's share thanks to the hastily written will. This was not usual but possible because Robert had to sell half the estate to Matthew (away from the entail, which legally ring-fenced an estate and its assets) to keep from going under. This happened increasingly, which is why entail was ultimately abolished. When Robert dies and leaves his share to George, George and his mother will be co-owners, which will certainly be unusual. Of course, there's always the spectre of Robert remarrying, should Cora die early, and suddenly producing a son. Which means the future of Mary's son is not yet absolutely certain.

Nevertheless, given the strong likelihood of inheriting Downton, George will be brought up always mindful of his future responsibilities and the work needed to keep the house going. It could be a heavy burden on such small shoulders. Sybbie's background creates a complication for her future of another kind: her mother was Lady Sybil, the beautiful youngest daughter of Lord Grantham, but her father is Tom Branson, an Irishman and former chauffeur, now land agent to the family.

Later, the questions surrounding their upbringing and what decisions ought to be made with regard to their education may become more complex, but for the moment they share a nursery and a nanny and, for all intents and purposes, are as brother and sister. We can well imagine that they will turn most naturally to each other for comfort and companionship throughout their lives, both understanding the extraordinary circumstances into which they were born in a way that few others will.

Although George will be brought up as an earl-in-waiting, his parents' marriage was a mixed one, just as Sybbie's parents' was. George's father was not born the heir to an earldom, he came into it quite unexpectedly as a young man in his twenties and brought with him his modish ideas about democracy, equality and fairness; it will be interesting to see whether his widow, Lady Mary, will decide to teach their son something of these values. Her own background is decidedly traditional and conformist, but she is of course living in a changing world and finds herself drawn to modern ideas now and then, almost against her will. Nor is she as tamed by conformity as she'd like to imagine – her own strength of character frequently wins the battle against the expectations of the past.

Sybbie is the child of rebellious parents and it is certain that Tom will wish to let her know of her Irish ancestry as well as his strong socialist ideals. However, he finds himself parallel to Mary, if travelling in the opposite direction – he is drawn to the old world and those that occupy it or, at least, he does not damn them as outright as he used to.

Matthew Crawley, father of George, is remembered on Mary's dressing-room table.

Baby Sybbie was christened a Catholic, much to her grandfather's chagrin.

Tom and Miss Sybbie Branson

For now, the nursery is a haven from the worries of the adult sphere and things are done here as they have been for several generations. To our modern eyes, the life of a child in the nursery under Nanny's jurisdiction seems almost unbearably harsh, but at the time this was seen to be in the child's best interests. For one thing, by living in the nursery at the top of the house, the infants were excused from the formalities of the drawing room and could behave as children. By way of example, in the nursery they would wear flannel and cotton clothes, but to go downstairs they would be dressed in highly starched, fussy outfits.

Of course, the children didn't tend to feel that they had been saved from the drawing room – on the contrary, they missed their parents and many grew up to realise they hardly knew them. In *Grace and Favour* Loelia Ponsonby describes a typical aristocratic childhood that may have chimed with Mary's, explaining that she and her peers spent their early years 'almost entirely in the society of servants… dumped in the nursery, which was as far away as possible, either on the top storey up a lot of stairs or in a remote wing with a green baize door across the corridor to protect the polite world from horrid noises'.

In these sorts of circumstances, the extended family of servants meant a great deal to a young child. The servants themselves would often have grown up as part of a large brood of siblings in a small house; they were used to the boisterousness of children and were, consequently, often more forgiving and affectionate. Nurses (the Nanny's assistants) and nannies were sometimes more loved than mothers, butlers as respected as fathers – as we see with Carson and Mary – and kitchen maids reliable sources of stolen biscuits. The parents rarely went into the nursery themselves and the children would be seen only for half an hour or an hour when brought downstairs, dressed in their best clothes and expected to behave impeccably. There was even a popular joke of the day about a mother who only recognised her infant in the park because she remembered the nurse.

NANNY
'Ah, are we too early?'

MARY
'Bring them in, Nanny. I don't think anyone will mind.'

CORA
'Your Papa might, but he isn't here to complain.'

Despite this, parents of the twentieth century believed that they were much nicer to their children than former generations had been. Julian's great-grandfather, John Wrightson, for example (who was president and principal of the Downton Agricultural College, and so provided the name for the show), disliked babies so much he established a house in the village, the Warren, and my wretched great-great-grandmother had to visit her babies there until they were allowed in the main house at the age of five or six. This was in the 1870s, hardly a thousand years ago.

Many parents justified their routine for the children with the latest fashion for scientific thinking: behaviourism. This was the rationale behind a popular belief in the 1920s that children could be trained to behave in desirable ways through suitable rewards and punishments.

The frequent consequence of only seeing their parents in these restricted surroundings was that the children rarely felt they could be themselves or talk truthfully to their mother or father. We all know the child – we may well have been the child – who chooses to shield their parents from any sad or bad reports, particularly if they don't see their parents much, so as to keep everything good humoured and happy.

Parents then, too, expected a certain amount of reverence from their children and perhaps weren't interested in them until they really had something to say. Julian reflects this in a line he gives to Robert, when Cora asks him to stay and see the children. 'Just as soon as they're able to answer back,' he replies.

In fact, Sybbie – the older of the two cousins – does reply to Robert, her grandfather, calling him 'Donk', which he doesn't much like. Alastair Bruce, Downton Abbey's historical adviser, recalls: 'The actress who plays Sybbie is like Shirley Temple – she gave three perfect takes one after another and delivered the ['Donk'] comic line with precision timing.'

But even with all the grandeur that parents and grandparents could muster, it was usually an accepted fact that Nanny was the one in charge – of the adults as well as the children. A mother would always ask Nanny first if it was convenient for her to take her own children out and even then Nanny would usually go with them, so that they were still in her charge.

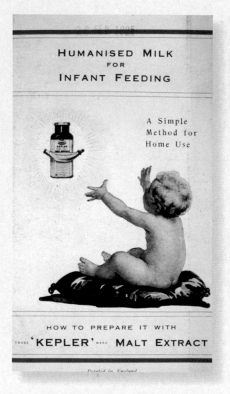

An advertisement for baby milk from 1925.

In the nursery, home remedies would be doled out for those feeling poorly – Kepler's Malt, cod liver oil and milk of magnesia were all kept in the cupboard. Bumps and bruises were treated with Pond's Extract and Pommade Divine, both of which sound suspiciously like face cream and hair oil and may have been similarly as effective. Food was delivered up to the nursery, but nannies and cooks famously fought, with furious notes sent downstairs: 'The children cannot be expected to eat this.' Nursery food was just as one might expect – soft, hot and milky. One woman recalled from her childhood 'a good deal of porridge, bread and butter, hot buttered toast and a great many milk puddings… On better days there was roly-poly (suet) pudding… and spotted dog, a suet-y sausage stuffed with currants. Also, treacle tart, pancakes, apple charlotte and the dizzy delight of chocolate eclairs.'

One nanny, when taking the children to stay at their grandparents' house, instructed the cook that her charges would eat 'porridge with thick cream… followed by bread which has been well soaked in whipped egg and then fried. On this they have little rolls of bacon. Mid-morning they have fruit… usually apple well shredded. Lunch at one sharp, they have jellied or clear soup, fish or chicken to follow then a milk pudding to finish. For tea at four o'clock, bread and butter, little sandwiches of jam and a sponge cake.' It all sounds rather delicious to me, but the children may not have had much choice as to whether or not they were going to eat it.

Stuffed with food, the babies would be rolled out for a walk in their perambulators dressed in – to our modern eyes – extraordinary outfits. Despite those past generations being used to freezing-cold houses (no central heating, remember), there seems to have been a real fear of a child catching a chill when they went outside. Whether hot or not, until 31 May, an infant would typically be dressed in a vest, a woolly binder (a sort of soft baby corset, to keep the tummy warm), mackintosh knickers over the cloth nappy, wool knickers, a voluminous starched petticoat, a robe and finally a pelisse (a long-sleeved cotton coat) with a big cape collar.

FRENCH TOAST

Comfort food for children and grown-ups alike, 'eggy bread'
is a great standby dish for breakfast, tea or indeed any other time of day.
Serve with bacon or fresh fruit, or spread with jam – or just as it is.

SERVES 1 ADULT
AND 2 CHILDREN

3 eggs
2 tablespoons milk
salt and pepper
butter, for frying
4 slices white bread
   (slightly stale is best)
icing sugar and cinnamon,
   for sprinkling

Crack the eggs into a wide, shallow bowl. Add the milk and whisk well with a fork. Season with salt and pepper.

Heat a frying pan over a medium heat and add a knob of butter. Slide a piece of bread into the egg mixture, coating it all over. When the butter is sizzling, place the eggy bread in the pan and fry for a few minutes on each side until golden. Repeat with the other slices of bread, adding more butter for frying if necessary.

Transfer the French toast on to plates, sprinkle with sugar and cinnamon and cut into triangles or fingers to serve.

PANCAKES

Traditionally eaten on Shrove Tuesday, pancakes are a way of using up any milk, butter and eggs in the house before the abstinence of Lent. These are the thin, French-style crêpes which were popularised in England in the eighteenth century.

MAKES 12–14

250g plain flour
a pinch of salt
2 eggs
600ml milk
butter, for frying
caster sugar and wedges
    of lemon, to serve

Sieve the flour and salt into a mixing bowl. Make a well in the middle of the flour and break the eggs into it. Add half the milk and start to whisk the eggs and milk with a balloon whisk, gradually incorporating the flour from the edges. Pour in the rest of the milk and carry on whisking until you have a smooth batter.

Heat a frying pan over a medium heat and add a knob of butter. Swirl it around until melted and then pour any excess into a saucer, leaving just a coating of grease in the pan.

When the pan is nice and hot (but not smoking), pour a ladleful of batter into the pan and tilt the pan from side to side so the batter runs evenly over the surface. As the pancake starts to set, lift the edges with a spatula and when it looks golden and lacy underneath (this should take no longer than a minute), flip it over using the spatula. Cook for less than a minute on the other side and then slide on to a warm plate.

Continue to cook the pancakes in this way and pile them up on the plate, covered with a clean tea towel to keep warm.

Serve with a squeeze of lemon and a sprinkling of sugar.

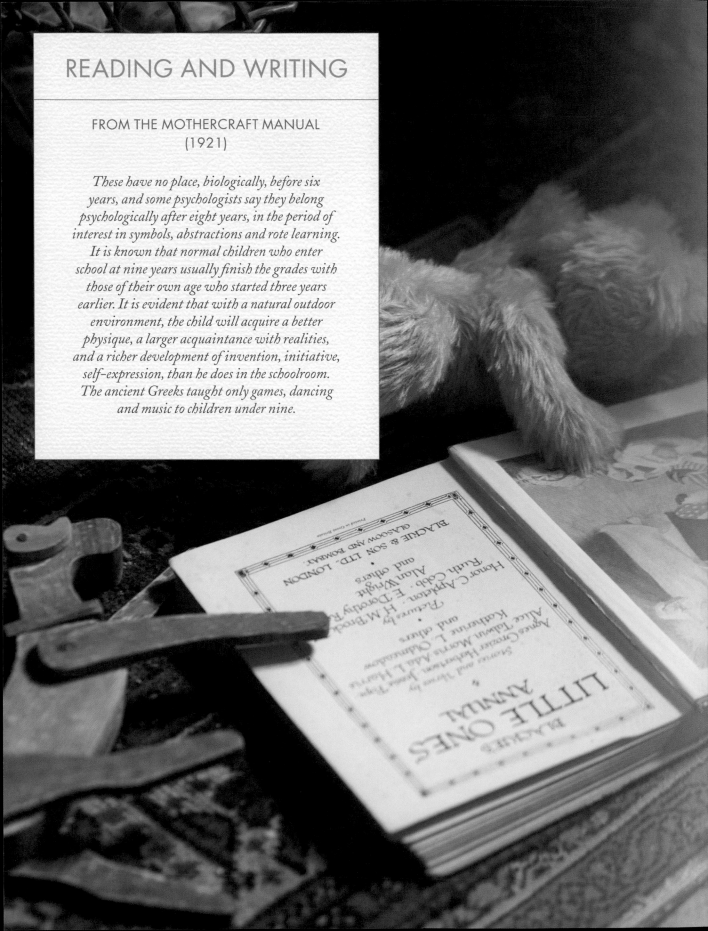

READING AND WRITING

FROM THE MOTHERCRAFT MANUAL (1921)

These have no place, biologically, before six years, and some psychologists say they belong psychologically after eight years, in the period of interest in symbols, abstractions and rote learning. It is known that normal children who enter school at nine years usually finish the grades with those of their own age who started three years earlier. It is evident that with a natural outdoor environment, the child will acquire a better physique, a larger acquaintance with realities, and a richer development of invention, initiative, self-expression, than he does in the schoolroom. The ancient Greeks taught only games, dancing and music to children under nine.

The nurseries themselves varied, of course, from house to house. Children's nursery furniture was expensive to buy but ravishing, such as elaborately built dolls' houses with their own custom-made exquisite furniture. In her memoir *A Nice Clean Plate* Lavinia Smiley tells us that the nursery at Parham had its own pantry, a lift to bring food from the kitchen, a telephone, a rocking horse, a piano and toys, clothes and medicines, 'all of it as bright and pleasant as could be'. You can see how some of these childishly pleasant nurseries, even the ones less elaborately tricked out, were preferable to the chilly atmosphere of the parents' drawing room.

All children must grow up and eventually Sybbie and George will need to be educated. Generally, children were educated at home until the boys were sent to boarding school at around the age of six or seven. Few aristocratic girls went to school, although some of the cleverer ones might have demanded it. Instead they were taught by governesses – a tradition that was beginning to die out by the 1930s, although not completely for some while after that.

It stands to reason that the education a girl received was only as good as the governess that taught them, and this standard varied wildly. While education for upper-class boys and young men had long been taken seriously in schools such as Eton, Winchester, Harrow and Ampleforth, that of the girls was less well established. Schools for girls were far from non-existent – there were some well-known good ones, such as Sherborne School and Cheltenham Ladies' College, as well as many Catholic convent schools – but they tended to focus on music, dancing, languages and social skills rather than aiming to get their pupils into university, where they might study medicine or law. Upper-class young 'gels' were still largely expected to acquire their position in life through their marriages rather than their careers. Of course, for many, after the First World War, marriage simply wasn't an option; the 1921 census made it clear – there were nearly two million more women than men. Yet, for the majority, their education had prepared them for little else. Despite this, in the 1920s, university became an increasingly popular option for the female sex – of the 1,679 people that obtained degrees in 1922, 20 per cent were women.

A watercolour sketch of Eton College, 1880.

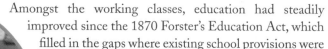

Amongst the working classes, education had steadily improved since the 1870 Forster's Education Act, which filled in the gaps where existing school provisions were inadequate. Constant amendments to educational law and discussions led by the likes of Keir Hardie, arguing that education should be free and open to all, encouraged many families to send their children to school. This meant that even the likes of Daisy, born at the very tail-end of the 1890s and the lowest of the low in the social scale, would have had basic literacy and numeracy skills.

In series five, we see Daisy embark on a new educational quest, aided by Miss Sarah Bunting, a schoolteacher in the village, played by Daisy Lewis. To prepare her part, the actress read a biography of Winifred Holtby, a progressive young woman from Yorkshire in the 1920s. 'So I put Sarah as well schooled but not upper class.

Sarah Bunting

I think she comes from a wealthy farming family, so she had governesses and could have gone to Oxford University,' she explains. 'I feel like Sarah represents a new class of that time, because she is highly educated but has taken on the socialist doctrines she was exposed to at university. Coupled with her experiences during the First World War, I think that's why she decides to return to the place she grew up. But it all also means she has been galvanised in her views about the landed gentry.'

Daisy's education would have been deliberately basic – it was called 'elementary education' because it aimed to teach only the fundamental elements of knowledge (the 'three Rs' – reading, writing and arithmetic) and nothing more; there was no intention of teaching the working classes in order that they may go on to further schooling. Despite good progress in education provision for children, there were still country schools well into the 1930s, taught by a single schoolmistress who presided over a room divided by a curtain, with the younger pupils in one half and the older children in the other. Most pupils left as soon as they legally could, to go and work in the fields – families could not afford to feed their own children otherwise. This is most likely to be the case with Daisy and it's a sad fact that her very cleverness could have led to her leaving school earlier rather than later, possibly hindering her own confidence in her intelligence as an adult.

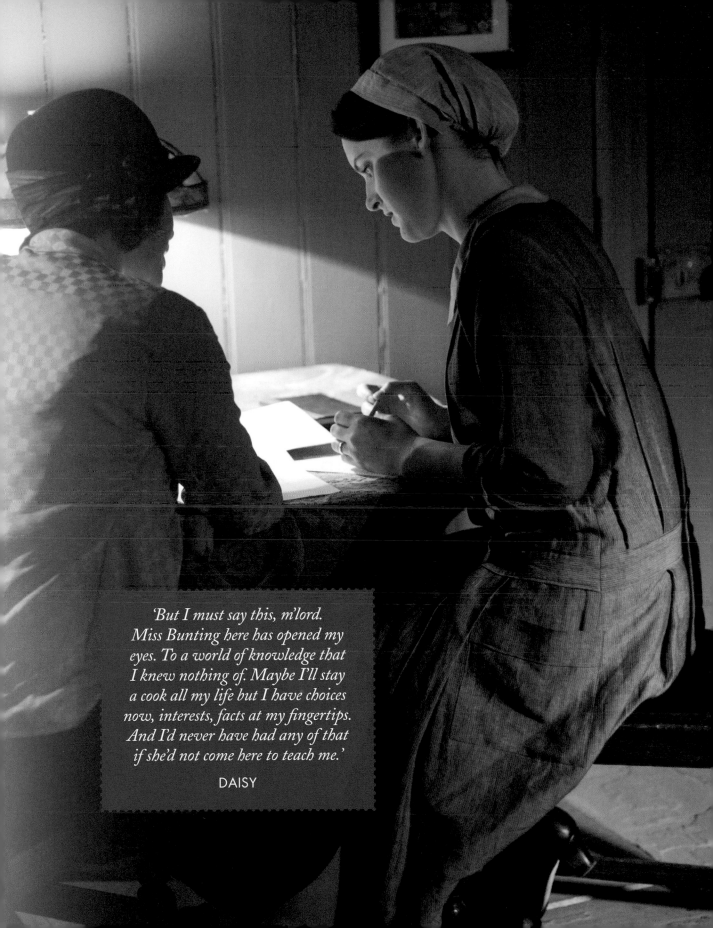

'But I must say this, m'lord. Miss Bunting here has opened my eyes. To a world of knowledge that I knew nothing of. Maybe I'll stay a cook all my life but I have choices now, interests, facts at my fingertips. And I'd never have had any of that if she'd not come here to teach me.'

DAISY

Will this be the plight of Edith's own daughter, Marigold? Eighteen months old now, Edith has taken her back from the adopted parents in Switzerland and placed her closer by, with the Drewe family, tenants of her father's farm. Only Tim Drewe, the farmer, is privy to the secret and only half the secret at that; although he has almost certainly guessed that Edith is the real mother, it hasn't been explicitly said.

We know that Edith weaned her own baby and it must have been unbearably hard for her to hand her daughter over to another couple; particularly as before 1926 there was no formal legal system of adoption. Edith could easily have lost all trace of her daughter and, equally, should her daughter have grown up and wished to find Edith, she would have found it almost impossible to do so. By placing Marigold with the Drewe family, Edith is ensuring that she is, at least, able to keep an eye on her. Nor should we judge Edith harshly for deciding not to keep her own child; illegitimacy was considered a stain upon both the mother's and the child's characters. Only in this way could she protect Marigold from being shunned by society, just as former maid Ethel took the same decision for her own Charlie.

Charlie – Ethel's boy.

EDITH

'I can't have her here. My parents disapproved of my friendship with her mother. They'd feel uncomfortable for the baby to be in the house.'

TIM DREWE

'I see.'

EDITH

'Which is why it has to be a secret. I hope I can make you understand how important that is.'

Edith holds her daughter, Marigold.

Andrew Scarborough (Tim Drewe) asked himself why his character would take on Edith's child: 'One reason is his loyalty to the estate and the way his father brought him up, as Lord Grantham's grateful tenants. I think he must have had wonderful parents as he is so fair and thinks with his heart. He's not stupid – he has a great deal of imagination to put himself in Lady Edith's shoes and not be judgemental.'

Andrew took inspiration from his own family background to colour in his character: 'I modelled him a little on my grandfather, who also had that gentle Yorkshire accent, using words like 'yonder'. Tim's warm, but it's difficult for him to show emotion. What is dark about the situation is that although [Tim] is probably getting attached to the baby, he would be the disciplinarian. If my grandfather wasn't pleased with you, you knew about it, despite the soft voice.' And there's more, demonstrating once again that *Downton Abbey* may be a television drama, but it has its roots in real life. 'My grandmother's sister had an illegitimate baby,' reveals Andrew. 'She was ostracised by the whole family – I think she ended up in a mental institution. My father wasn't even aware that he had another aunt for years, as she was never talked about, and we still don't know what happened to her. And my grandmother on my mother's side had a baby with a GI and gave it to her sister to bring up.'

Andrew enjoyed filming with the children, although he admits that it can affect the way he might play a scene: 'It's quite difficult when you have to do a tense, argumentative scene, but then again, it's more realistic, as you have to express what you want without shouting and do it under your breath.'

Laura Carmichael laughs when I ask her about acting with the children: 'It's always a challenge because they're children and they're not exactly dying to be at work! But they have been great and there have been some magic moments.'

Daisy

VALENTINE'S DAY CARDS

TO MY VALENTINE

I WONDER CUPID
WHEN ON THE HUNT
WILL YOU CAPTURE
THE ONE I WANT.

The tradition of sending Valentine's cards on
14 February would be welcomed by servants who
had scant opportunity otherwise to reveal romantic
intentions under the watchful eyes of the butler
and housekeeper. Cards were always supposed to
be signed anonymously, however, leaving plenty of
room for misunderstandings in the servants' hall…

FOOD

Six times a day in Downton Abbey, a full meal is served: two breakfasts, two lunches, two dinners. Three for the servants and three for the family. Not to mention two afternoon teas, with all the homemade bread, cakes and biscuits they would involve. Backbreaking work for Mrs Patmore and her kitchen assistants… and just as hard work for Lisa Heathcote, *Downton Abbey*'s food stylist.

In 1924 the fashion was for highly decorated food – even the edges of the serving platters would be garnished with thinly cut slices of radish or strewn with the verdant colours of watercress – and aspic, a clear liquid that could be set in pretty moulds with, say, a tiny strand of dill perfectly suspended within. A gelatin made from meat stock, aspic is, for most modern tastes, absolutely revolting to eat – like a solid consommé – but it created a beautiful effect in the 1920s dining room. For Lisa's purposes, aspic is wonderful to work with, as it stays set and glossy even after hours under hot studio lights.

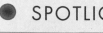

A pie is prepared in Mrs Patmore's kitchen.

Lisa's biggest challenge with the food is continuity. Not just the long hours that it takes to film the dining scenes, but the fact that the kitchen and dining room are separated by sixty miles. Filming is done in blocks in each location, which means the footmen will leave Mrs Patmore's kitchen in Ealing with a platter to emerge in the dining room at Highclere some three weeks later.

When planning the food for a scene, Lisa has to take on board several factors. First and foremost, she has to think seasonally. Not everything out of season is completely off limits; by 1924, a house such as Downton would be ordering things such as oranges and lemons from the bigger stores in York, as well as occasional luxuries from Harrods and Fortnum's in London. The grander houses of that time would also often have hothouses in which exotic fruits such as pineapple would be cultivated – these were notoriously difficult to grow and so were a real triumph for a house to present during a dinner party. But on the whole, if a scene is set in February, then Lisa can't include ingredients that are too obviously seasonal, such as salmon and strawberries.

Secondly, Lisa establishes from the script which course the characters are eating when the action takes place. For a grand dinner, there might be as many as nine courses

– soup, hors d'oeuvres, roast, entrée, pudding, savoury – although each portion would be quite modest.

For recipe ideas, Lisa went to the National Archives to look at private house menus. These are full of inspiration, but are largely written in French, as was the fashion, so Lisa found herself turning to Nancy Lake's *Menus Made Easy: How to Order Dinner and Give the Dishes Their French Names*, which was published in 1891 and ran to several editions. Doubtless, the likes of Mrs Patmore and Daisy would have found it invaluable in boosting their schoolgirl French. Lisa also uses cookbooks common to the period, such as those by Larousse, Mrs Beeton, Mrs Marshall and Elizabeth Rafferty. 'Downton's not changing too much and I like to use books they would have had in the kitchen, even if they were a little old-fashioned by then,' says Lisa. 'It's still very much a country house. But the new kitchen equipment has started to make a difference – a toaster for breakfast and a beater for soufflés and mousse.'

Using these recipes, Lisa is able to plan the food as carefully as the best country house cook – nothing that appears on a plate is there by accident. Even the platter decorations are put to good use, providing something light and easy for the actors to nibble on. When dining-room scenes take between ten and twelve hours to film, the actors soon learn not to be chewing any chicken in their shot, or they'll be chewing it for a long time and it won't taste so nice by the end of the day. Sometimes, though, hunger overcomes them. 'The worst is when we're filming a breakfast scene,' says Chris Croucher, producer. 'The actors arrive on set hungry, having been picked up from their houses at 7 a.m. or earlier. They can't help but start tucking into the sausages that have been put on their plates. The problem comes when they have to return to the scene after lunch. They're not so hungry anymore, but they still have to keep eating...'

Food is also an important element in the kitchen, where Mrs Patmore and Daisy are kept constantly busy. A house that size would have had a still room, with its own still-room maid, leading off the kitchen, in which the jams, jellies and cakes were made and tea-trays would be laid out. But for dramatic purposes it was decided to keep all the cooking action in the main room itself. Lisa and the set-dresser decide what Daisy and the other maids can be doing in each scene, taking the need for colour on the table – a bowl of lemons or leeks, for example – and the time of day into consideration. 'We keep them away from knives,' laughs Lisa. Baskets of vegetables are often seen sitting on the worktops – these are freshly bought before being dusted with handfuls of earth, kept in a bag by the art department, to give them that 'just out of the kitchen garden' look appropriate for 1924.

All the food is prepped by Lisa at her home, where she has an industrial kitchen, which means she also has to think about what food can travel, as well as the fact that it's hard to keep anything hot. 'It's creating an art form,' says Lisa. 'It's not about the eating, it's the look of it, and I really enjoy that.'

Elaborate food presentation was the order of the day.

MARCH
Farming

MARCH

In March the estate lies quiet. It is, perhaps, the least pretty time of year – grey and cold, the sodden mud clinging to Tom's boots as he tramps across the land, on his way to inspect the pigs or a tenant's cottage.

But as a countryman, he'll see something different: he knows the promise of a bountiful year begins with the spread of slurry on the fields. The calving and lambing has begun. The farm is cleaned up, fences are fixed, holes are plugged, ready for spring to be sprung.

An estate such as Downton Abbey with thousands of acres would have both tenant farmers and farmland of its own, being, in effect, self-sustaining. From the home farm, Mrs Patmore receives all the beef, chicken, pork and vegetables she needs, as well as having free rein over a number of herbs from the kitchen garden.

In many estates there would be a hothouse, producing tomatoes, lemons and peaches, as well as unusual and exotic fruits. There's certainly a Downton dairy too, providing the house's milk, butter and cheese. This wasn't unusual – the Astors of Cliveden even took their own milking cow with them when they went up to Scotland.

The rented-out arable land would customarily be divided into fields of around a hundred acres each, with crop rotation the common method of growing: wheat or winter oats, followed by half clover for hay and half feed for sheep – rye, winter barley, swedes and kale; followed by turnips. 'This rotation was as unalterable as the law of Medes and Persians,' wrote A. G. Street in his moving memoir, *Farmer's Glory*, about life on the farm at the start of the twentieth century. 'Any slight variation was considered a sin... One didn't farm for cash profits but did one's duty by the land.'

As well as farmland, an estate would have woods and gardens for pleasure, whether for raising game for shoots or growing flowers for the dining table.

Pleasure gardens could be extraordinarily elaborate, making them a draw for any summer party, with rockeries, lakes, tennis courts and croquet lawns. While beautiful gardens were the pride of any estate, it was only the employed workers that actually held a trowel or planted a bulb. Gardening might be something we like to do today, but it was classed as servants' work in 1924 (the fashion for getting one's hands dirty did not begin until after about 1930), as one can read between the lines when Lord Merton replies to Lady Shackleton, after she asks him how his lovely garden is: 'Still lovely. Largely because I have the same lovely gardener.' The hierarchy of responsibility for the garden was so strict that many châtelaines feared being told off by their head gardeners – who were highly skilled workers – for so much as picking their own peaches off a tree. There's a wonderful story from Loelia Ponsonby, of her orchid expert, when she was married to the Duke of Westminster: '[He] lived in hopes of producing a marvellous new cross that would be worth hundreds of pounds and we sympathised with him when he came and complained that his most precious bloom, a pure white virgin veiled in white cellophane to keep away pollen-carrying insects, had been picked by Lord Carnarvon and presented to a girlfriend.' The descendant of that Lord Carnarvon, of course, owns Highclere Castle.

It's not so hard to understand why, until the twentieth century, a man's influence and power were not measured by his job, his wife, his friends, his money or even his title – although all of these things helped – but mainly by his land. The landowners were the country's principal players for hundreds of years, the long period when a vast acreage indicated both riches and influence. To be 'landed gentry' indicated that you came from an old landowning family and could live off the money earned from your tenant farmers. This income could be considerable: at the end of the nineteenth century, the Duke of Buccleuch earned £217,000 a year from 460,000 acres. But even the smaller estates were nothing to sneeze at: the Duke of Marlborough got by on £37,000 a year from 24,000 acres. This at a time when the average working-class family income was less than a £100 a year.

MARY

'I love the view from up here.'

BRANSON

'If you know the view, all the better. Follow that hedge, to the left of it is Oakwood Farm, to the right is all farmed by us.'

But as the nineteenth century turned, so did the tide against the landowners. Land, having been considered the safest and most prestigious investment of all, turned out not to be so. There were agricultural depressions, the constant threat of cheaper imports and ever-increasing taxation. Still, up to a point, these things could be borne by the aristocracy.

Rt. Hon. David Lloyd George, Prime Minister 1916-1922

In the years immediately after the war, there was a certain air of prosperity and many tenants bought the farm they had previously rented. This created a new breed of owner-occupiers, which shifted the landscape agriculturally, economically and politically, coming as they did at the same time as changes in the mechanisation of farming, a dramatic reduction in government subsidies and the growth of motorcar ownership.

The demise of the power of the landed gentry meant that politicians lost interest in agriculture, particularly if it meant maintaining the old patrician order. In 1920, Lloyd George introduced a new zero per cent capital gains tax on land sales, which encouraged owners to reduce their estates by converting a highly taxable income into a tax-free sale. This was surely a deliberate move by the prime minister to break up the estates. The point is that all these great estates had been borne out of a pre-taxation era: if you had land, you could live off it by renting it out or farming it, or both, with no taxes to pay. The introduction of taxation was not just a heavy burden – it was their ultimate destruction. By 1922, a quarter of all agricultural land had been sold. Nor was it all kept as farmland – in 1918 there were twelve million acres under cultivation; by 1926, this had fallen to nine million.

ROBERT: *'You do realise we can sell land as a capital gain and pay no tax on it at all?'*

MARY: *'And end up with an estate that can't support the house.'*

So great estates were broken up, country houses were sold off and the newly formed (1908) National Union of Farmers – which forbade landowners from joining – was the strongest body in agriculture, with ten thousand members (only a paltry number of farmers sat in Parliament). For many, it felt as if the decline of the aristocracy was in freefall.

Those landowners and new owner-occupiers who held on had to diversify or die. This is what we see happening in *Downton Abbey* in series four, with the Granthams' additional problem of a large death duties bill following the loss of Matthew. This could not be easily settled, thanks to the law of entail. This was the system devised to prevent future generations from squandering their inheritance: a grandfather would legally settle the family estates on to his grandson so that the son would only ever have interest in them during his lifetime, with access to income but not capital.

'Since I own the other half of everything, isn't it more appropriate for me to manage the boy's fortunes?'

ROBERT

The law of entail was effectively abolished in 1925 with the Settled Land Act, but many families continued to operate their inheritance in this way, understanding as they did that it had protected aristocratic estates for centuries. But in 1924, our Downton year for the opening of the fifth series, this system was still legally intact.

At the time of his death, Matthew owned half of the Downton estate (having bought it out using his inheritance from Swire), while Robert owns the other half. When Matthew apparently died with no will, it was believed that his assets would transfer almost entirely to George, bypassing Mary (her small share is only a life interest). Added to this, Robert is keen to be the sole person in charge of the entire estate again – in other words, controlling his and Matthew's halves as he once did before he had to sell out.

Fortunately, the discovery of the letter – tucked into a book in his office – in which Matthew named Mary as his sole heir ensures that she now owns his half of the estate; it is this she seeks to protect on behalf of their son. Still, it doesn't dodge the question of the high death duties (taxes levied on inherited property) that need to be paid and now she and Robert have to find a way to pay them without breaking up the estate if George is to inherit Downton Abbey intact. (Death duties will have to be paid again when Robert dies, so they need to make sure there is money to spare.) Furthermore, Robert is not keen to relinquish control to his daughter.

'My destiny is to save Downton for George.'

MARY

It is now that we see Mary's true mettle. Despite her old-fashioned outlook in many ways – she does not fundamentally disagree with the order of the world and is far less a suffragette than Edith, let alone Sybil – at this point, she begins to be attracted to the idea that she herself might be the protector of her son's inheritance. The question is whether she decides to protect it in the traditional way, through a second suitable marriage to a man with money and power of his own, which would stabilise Downton, or in a radical new way, through industry and modern farming methods.

The 1920s were a constant battle of trying to outwit the weather, machinery, interest rates and the world markets – a battle the farmer often lost. Many landowning families did not manage to find a solution to the difficulties they faced, but Mary is pragmatic. Together with Tom, as the land agent, and occasionally with Robert's backing, she works to find new ways for the estate to yield money. Pig farming is one such idea.

ROBERT: *'Crop rotation? Livestock versus cereals? Indeed, the whole matter of the tax. There are lots of things I'd like your opinion on.'*

MARY: *'I assume you're trying to make some sort of point.'*

CORA: *'He's trying to show that a woman's place is in the home.'*

At this point in our story, Charles Blake enters the fray, a rather handsome knight in tweed, although Mary doesn't see him that way at first. He is part of a government investigation into how the breaking up of estates may affect food production, something that was indeed happening at the time. Diversification from arable farming into livestock was a big risk, particularly as improvements in refrigeration meant that cheap meat started to be imported from abroad. Nor do the Granthams appear to be starting slowly: they have embarked on intensive farming with pigs, managed by Mr Drewe. The recent discovery of vitamin supplements – allowing animals to be raised indoors – makes this a new method and, therefore, pretty risky. If it all goes wrong, Mary and Tom's bright idea could be responsible for losing a great deal of money.

Charles
Blake

ROSAMUND: *'I gather you've launched into pigs these days.'*

BRANSON: *'Yes. And their arrival was quite the adventure in which Mr Blake and Mary were the hero and heroine.'*

Tom's role as land agent is crucial to the success of the estate. A land agent, sometimes called a steward, traditionally was the man (and it always was a man) who supervised the business affairs of an estate, from the farming to the collecting of the rents. He would be treated as a privileged and senior servant. So in some ways, this puts Tom in a funny position – he is from below stairs, now above stairs as widower of the family's daughter and essentially works as a servant once more. Hence Violet's confusion: 'I thought that I could call him Branson again now he's the agent.' But his experience from the farm in Ireland, his trustworthiness, his energy for new ideas and his friendship with Mary should stand the estate in good stead (so long as it works out with the pigs).

The outdoor scenes on the estate are largely shot at the Highclere Castle location itself, which is nothing enviable. The crew have a saying that when it's warm elsewhere, it's cold at Highclere; and when it's cold elsewhere, it's freezing. Julian Ovenden, who plays Charles Blake, however, did enjoy filming the pig scenes, despite the mud: 'They were very juicy scenes. Usually one has to concentrate and be very economical and specific, as you only have a few lines to establish your character.'

The infamous pig scene in series four, in which Mary and Charles spend the night giving water to the dehydrated pigs and end up very muddy in the process, was in fact filmed during the day. 'By that point we were shooting in high summer,' explains producer Chris Croucher, 'so to film at night would have put our schedule out. Julian rewrote what was originally an exterior scene as an interior so that it could take place in a barn. An enormous tent was put over the barn to black it out and then we had to create the wet mud. We had to use clean soil as there was a lot of throwing it around near the actors' mouths. We also had to be very careful around the pigs as they can be quite vicious!'

The great revelation about Charles is that he turns out to come from an aristocratic background, something that the actor wasn't aware of when he accepted the part: 'I knew that they wanted someone who was a match for Mary, but who embodied a slightly more liberal point of view that would clash with her and the family's politics. [When I found out he was upper class] it was rather nice – I don't think I would have played any scene any differently, in retrospect. He's a free-thinker and modern for that time. He believes women have as much right to free thought as men. Perhaps he even feels burdened by being an aristocrat, in line for an inheritance and a big estate in Ireland, not needing any money. I think he wants to forge his own path rather than rely on his family – that's his driving force.'

Of his character's admiration for Mary, Julian Ovenden says: 'They have similarities between them. They're both quite dominant and speak their mind, but are actually quite practical when it comes down to it. I also think he finds her frustratingly mysterious. She wrong-foots him, she's obviously intelligent and very capable, which he finds attractive.'

Andrew Scarborough plays the estate's long-standing tenant farmer, Tim Drewe – his family have rented land from Downton Abbey since King George IV was on the throne, a hundred years before, as Robert likes to remind Mary. Andrew was also unsure as to how his character would play out in the show: 'When I joined there was always the possibility that I'd come back, so for the first few days I felt as if I was auditioning! But I was delighted when I found out that something meaty was going to happen.' Tim, of course, is more than just a farmer with some knowledge of pigs – he takes in Edith's secret daughter, Marigold, to raise with his other children. This gives his storyline a complex layer – he is both an equal of Edith in this situation and her family's tenant, which means a level of deference to them. It has meant that there are sometimes complications: 'I was doing a scene with Lady Edith and didn't want to take my cap off, because I felt it would be too distracting. And he's caught in the middle, trying to advise her on something about the daughter. We came to the conclusion that he wouldn't have his hat on at the start. Little things like that, you have to think through.'

Farming in the 1920s was a tough business to be in and it wasn't going to get any easier – quite the opposite, in fact – for some years yet. But with Mary and Tom's determination to make the land work for them, combined with Robert's kind-hearted attitude towards the tenants, they should be able to ensure the house's livelihood, so that it may continue to stand proud for generations to come. That is their purpose and their driving force. For the Crawleys, Downton Abbey is not just bricks and mortar, but is as much a part of them as their own flesh and blood. Perhaps that is hard for us to understand today, but life then was lived less for oneself than on behalf of unknown, as yet unborn, descendants. It might have made the aristocracy appear cold at times, as they had to make ruthless decisions to support the future rather than the present. But it makes for a rather compelling television show, as I'm sure you will agree.

IRISH STEW

A simple and hearty stew to remind Tom Branson of home, this is good country cooking.
This variation uses lamb instead of the more traditional mutton.

SERVES 6

a few tablespoons vegetable oil or dripping
900g stewing lamb, cut into large chunks
12 shallots, peeled and left whole
2 celery stalks, sliced
3 carrots, cut into chunks
100g pearl barley
1 bay leaf
small bunch of thyme, leaves picked
1 litre vegetable stock
salt and pepper
900g potatoes, peeled and cut into large chunks
a knob of butter
chopped parsley, to serve

Preheat the oven to 180°C/350°F/gas 4.

Heat the oil or fat in a large casserole dish over a high heat. Add the lamb and toss in the fat until browned. Remove the meat with a slotted spoon and set aside on a plate.

Add another tablespoon of oil or fat to the pot, followed by the shallots, celery, carrots, pearl barley, bay leaf and thyme leaves. Cook over a medium heat for about 10 minutes until the onions have softened. Return the meat to the dish and pour over the stock. Season well with salt and pepper.

Put the potatoes on top of the stew, cover the pot and cook in the oven for 1½ hours until the potatoes are soft and the meat is tender. Top up with a little stock if the stew starts to dry out.

Stir the butter into the stew and sprinkle with parsley to serve.

EVE'S PUDDING

This comforting apple pudding, with its sponge topping, makes good use of English Bramleys. In autumn you can add a handful of freshly picked blackberries to the apples.

SERVES 6

700g Bramleys or other cooking apples
75g demerara sugar
a large pinch of freshly grated nutmeg
zest of 1 lemon
75g butter, plus extra for greasing
75g caster sugar, plus extra for sprinkling
1 egg, beaten
125g self-raising flour
2–3 tablespoons milk

Preheat the oven to 180°C/350°F/gas 4. Grease a 900ml ovenproof dish with butter.

Peel and core the apples and slice thinly. Place in the prepared dish and sprinkle the demerara sugar, nutmeg and lemon zest over them. Add 1 tablespoon of water.

In a separate bowl, cream the butter and caster sugar until light and fluffy. Add the egg gradually, beating well. Sift the flour into the bowl and fold into the mixture. Add a splash of milk – enough to give a dropping consistency. Spread this mixture over the apples.

Bake in the oven for 40–50 minutes, until the sponge mixture is golden and firm to the touch in the centre. Sprinkle with caster sugar and serve with custard or cream.

LOCATIONS

While Ealing Studios is the home of the *Downton Abbey* production offices, wardrobe and prop stores, as well as the built sets for the servants' quarters and the family's bedrooms, the lavish stateliness that we associate with the show comes from its locations. At the centre of these is Highclere Castle, the privately owned home of the Earl and Countess of Carnarvon, and the setting for the Crawley family.

Walking up to the castle is not always the romantic jaunt you think it might be – sitting high up on a hill, the wind catches you from all directions and it's not long before you have your head down, eyes streaming, coat collar pulled as tight as it will go. It makes one rather less envious of past inhabitants, living there without central heating and plumbed hot water. But walking through the castle's front door, the thing that hits you first is the realisation that it really is Downton Abbey. How you see it on the screen is pretty much how it is in real life.

Donal Woods, the production designer, explains his team's responsibility: 'We have to keep it familiar. Since 1912 the costumes have changed, but we have to embrace the permanence of the house. We might lighten the colours a little as we head into the 1920s, but it really is all still the same. From my point of view, until we get to 1925 and the Paris Exhibition, when Art Deco turns up, nothing has changed for years. Country houses didn't change – the family isn't going to suddenly go mad and have pink walls – and when the war came, no one was thinking about redesigning the wallpaper.'

Mrs Crawley's house, Bampton village.

Highclere Castle is not a purpose-built set and so the crew must behave slightly differently here than in Ealing Studios. Before one reaches the sweeping drive at the front of the house, several crew trucks and actors' trailers (more like caravans than Winnebagos) are parked on the lawn. Close to the front door is a table with tea and coffee – nothing, apart from bottled water, may be eaten or drunk inside. Spare lights, cables and camera tracks – these are used for above-stairs scenes to create a smoother sensation; for below stairs, they use hand-held cameras, giving a greater sense of movement and activity – alert one to the fact that you're on set, but you cannot help but be struck by the interior of the house itself. From the grand hall, with the various coats of arms of past wives of the Carnarvon earls around the gallery, to the hundreds of leather-bound books in the library and the pretty pink sofas in the drawing room, it looks exactly as you would expect, although the 'Please do not sit on here' printed cards placed on chairs remind you that these are real heirlooms, not imitations made by the art department. The house is in fact increasingly used by the Carnarvon family for their own enjoyment (they also have a cottage on the estate in which they live when the main house is hired out) and always when hosting a house party or shooting party for friends.

I watch the monitor as the director for episodes four and five, Minkie Spiro, shoots a scene with Michelle Dockery and Hugh Bonneville. There is absolute hush when the cameras are rolling – the slightest footfall on a creaky floorboard or muttered whisper will echo. Removing sound from the film is one of the production's more painstaking tasks: 'It's amazing how much of the twenty-first century we hear and edit out – at the time, you don't even know you can hear the distant sounds of the A34,' explains Liz Trubridge.

The scene wraps and the actors for the next scene begin rehearsing. Elizabeth McGovern (Cora), rather disconcertingly dressed in a pink fluffy dressing-gown, hairnet and Ugg boots, holds her script and blocks her movements, an industry phrase for working out exactly where she will stand and move to within the scene. A splendidly dressed, tall and booming Richard E. Grant introduces himself to me – 'Hi, I'm Richard' – and he looks so absolutely as if he has stepped out of 1924 that I am quite flummoxed and manage only, I am sure, a rather stupid reply.

But Highclere is only part of the story. Bampton in Oxfordshire is the location for any village scenes, right down to the churchyard where Lady Sybil and Matthew Crawley are buried. Donal says that they try to film there in blocks, so that it is less disruptive to the inhabitants, but the seasons are a factor in the schedule: 'There's a danger that we leave Highclere in winter and arrive at Bampton in spring, as the changes can be so quick, with hawthorn bushes in flower and trees blossoming almost from one day to the next.'

Bampton is also the village where the exterior of Isobel Crawley's house is filmed (the interior is a house in Beaconsfield, Buckinghamshire, and reflects the tastes of her progressive, intelligentsia outlook). The real-life owner takes great pride in her garden, now frequently admired by fans of the show from America to China, peering over the wall.

Violet's house is Byfleet Manor in Surrey. The design is more deliberately Edwardian inside, symbolic of her resistance to change. Lady Rosamund's house is in London's Belgrave Square – on the outside; the inside is the very pretty interior of West Wycombe, home to Sir Edward Dashwood and his family today.

For the inside of the Crawley family's London palace, seen for the first time in series four, Donal chose Basildon Park, a National Trust property close to Pangbourne: 'We had to find a house that was lavish, but not as lavish as Highclere. Basildon Park is a reasonable size, but not too enormous. We dressed it with some personal items, but it was its own Georgian interior that was right for the part.'

The grounds of Basildon Park were also used for the filming of the Hyde Park picnic scene in the final episode of series four. They had a rather unusual interruption to filming when a hot-air balloon that was running low on fuel made an unexpected landing right between the picnic and the crew trucks!

The London servants' quarters are another specially built set at Ealing, done, explains Donal, 'slightly more modern than Downton, with cream ceramic brick tiles in the kitchen and all rather smaller, to show that the space would be a bit tighter in a London house'.

Lady Rosamund's house, West Wycombe Park.

APRIL

Travel

APRIL

In our world today, with 24-hour television, social media and the internet giving any one of us a glimpse – or more – into the lives of others all around the globe at the mere push of a button or click of a mouse, it's hard to overstate just how exotic 'Abroad' was a hundred years ago.

Foreign countries were steeped in a culture almost entirely different from one's own, whether it was the clothes they wore, food they ate, god(s) they worshipped or language they spoke. Almost nothing, if you travelled overseas, was familiar.

What's more, only a very few people travelled. It took so long to get anywhere that you had to be prosperous enough not to need to be at home to do your job or work your farm for a period of time. (The only non-rich people who travelled went on a one-way ticket, whether as an exiled criminal or hopeful emigrant.) Until the early twentieth century, long-distance travel for the purpose of pleasure, whether across Britain or overseas, was almost entirely the preserve of the upper classes and the moneyed.

The Crawleys may be a family living in the northern provinces but, as aristocrats, several of their previous generations would have enjoyed the benefits of travel. By which I mean, the getting there as much as the arrival. Julian remembers his great-aunt Isie saying to him once: 'I always feel sad that your generation has missed the pleasure of travel.' To which he replied, 'Are you mad? We travel more than you ever did.' 'I don't mean the pleasure of getting there. I mean the pleasure of travel.' 'I am inclined to think she was right,' says Julian now.

Violet recalls travelling to St Petersburg in Russia in her youth, sometime around the 1870s, which would have seemed fabulously outlandish – 'glittering parades and rides in a horse-drawn sleigh, flying across the snow at midnight'.

In upper-class tradition, Robert almost certainly would have completed a Grand Tour as a young man, travelling all over Europe to educate himself in the great art and architecture of France, Italy, Spain and beyond. Cora, of course, came across

*Advertisement
for the Orient Express.*

from America in the 1880s as a young Buccaneer (the name given to heiresses who travelled to Europe in the hope of landing a titled husband). Even their daughters, whose own travel plans may have been rather curtailed by the First World War, manage to leave the shores of Britain: Mary motoring through the South of France for her honeymoon with Matthew; Edith, rather less happily, travelling to Switzerland. Even Sybil lived in Ireland for a while – not so exotic, perhaps, but a change of scenery at least.

The servants, however, are unlikely to have travelled much more than between their home village and Downton. Except during the war which, conversely for the men, provided the greatest opportunity for the working classes to travel. We know Bates was in the Second Boer War, which was fought in South Africa. But Anna admits she had never even been as far as Scotland before travelling there as Mary's lady's maid. This was one reason senior positions as valets and lady's maids were so coveted: Rosina Harrison, lady's maid to Lady Astor at Cliveden, chose her career because of her long-held urge to travel. There wasn't any other way for a working-class girl to do so, even though, for Rosina, it meant expensive training and the sacrifice of never having a husband and family.

Happily, by 1924, things were looking up for those who wished to see other places without spending several days on the journey. In the previous century trains had revolutionised the country in almost every aspect of life. Heavy goods could now be freighted with ease and people could begin to live further away from their work – the word 'commuter' started to come into use in the 1860s. As the national network grew, it became possible to have seaside holidays without an agonisingly slow journey there by horse and cart. Servants could get home to visit their families more than once a year without having to rely on a sporadic series of lifts and 'dog-carts'. It was even possible to get away for a 'weekend' if one worked. Gareth Neame, Julian Fellowes and the director Brian Percival deliberately chose to open *Downton Abbey*'s first ever episode with shots of John Bates sitting in a train, on his way to the house, a telegram speeding its way overhead in parallel – it demonstrated that this was not a Jane Austen world of candlelight and tapestries; a period drama, yes, but a period that shares elements with today's modern world, from trains and electricity, to mortgages and motor cars.

Mr Bates

Lady Edith
Crawley

Bicycles, too, had changed the way the working classes got around. For the first time, it was possible to travel faster than walking pace in an affordable manner (only the well-off could afford to hire a horse and carriage; only the rich could afford to keep one). By 1895, bicycles were commonplace amongst the young and less wealthy and working-class families soon aspired to the new motor-bicycles and sidecars.

At the end of the nineteenth century, too, came the motor car: slowly at first (quite literally), but increasingly fashionable amongst the well-to-do after the Motor Car Act of 1903 allowed speeds of 20 mph. In 1904 there were 8,000 registered car owners. After the First World War, mass-produced and relatively cheap motor cars were made and ownership grew at a steady rate: from 132,000 in 1914 to 1,715,000 motor vehicles registered in 1926. There were also a high number of motor-car fatalities, thanks to novice drivers (and no driving test) and pedestrians unused to speeding hulks of metal coming round the corner: 2.9 fatalities per thousand vehicles in 1926. Today, there are 0.1 fatalities per thousand. One statistic could give an extraordinary view of technology if misinterpreted: in 1904, during off-peak periods, a motor-driven cab would travel in central London at an average of 12 mph. Today, the average off-peak vehicle speed is recorded as 10 mph.

While the rich initially employed chauffeurs to drive them around, as we saw with the Crawleys and Tom Branson, when cars became more affordable, driving became a leisure pursuit of the rather more sporting and daring. Edith's ability to drive a car marks her out as very racy, in all senses of the word. Violet, however, refuses to sit in the front beside the driver.

There's a touching description of a passenger new to motor cars by A. G. Street. He writes about taking his reluctant father out, a man who greatly preferred his horse and trap: 'Anything over fifteen miles per hour was considered speeding, and I drove that car for several months to the accompaniment of "Steady! Steady!" For a long time he still sat forwards going uphill, and sat back with his feet braced against the footboards when going downhill.'

It's Tom Branson and Edith who best encapsulate all that travel has to offer and it's no coincidence that they are the two that drive the cars. For Tom, becoming a chauffeur enabled him to leave Ireland and find himself work other than the farm labouring that was probably his only real option back home. And then, of course, it meant that he met Sybil and was travelling not just in the physical sense, but across the classes too – up the stairs and through the green baize door, to live as one of the family. As we have seen, he learns that this is easier said than done. Tom suffers a dilemma – he lives 'above stairs' but is unlikely to find another earl's daughter who would want to marry him; nor can he find a nice Irish girl and take her back to live at Downton. As Julian says, 'It's all fine when he's in the family circle, but the moment a stranger comes in, it's revealed not to be OK. I think that's always true of a mésalliance.'

EDITH: *'So did you enjoy it? After all?'*

BRANSON: *'I've enjoyed it fine, but we must stand up to them, you and I. We may love them, but if we don't fight our corner, they'll roll us out flat.'*

Edith, meanwhile, is a young woman who has not enjoyed the best of good fortune in her life so far. 'For most of us, our lives are a combination of good and bad luck,' says Gareth Neame. 'Some of our friends may appear blissfully lucky – they are charmed; some are incredibly unlucky. Edith is a bad-luck person.' Edith is not alone in her generation in having her expectations of life turned completely inside out by the changes wrought by the war, but watching her navigate those stormy waters is blackly compelling. 'Hers is not the journey of a star beauty,' says Julian. 'Every time she does something, they keep changing the rules. She got pushed around by the war, but she makes a progression in spite of herself.'

Laura Carmichael agrees with this assessment of her character: 'She might have been the most conventional of the three sisters, but it didn't work out that way for her,' she says. 'She wants something for herself and she has the confidence that being a "lady" affords you. I feel as if, when she was growing up, she was always excluded, in the background reading a book. But it made her thoughtful and smart. When it came to the newspaper column, she was intimidated at first, but she found herself a role.'

AY 2524

Learning to drive a car and a tractor (something of a challenge for the actress, who has yet to take her driving test), having an affair with a married man and becoming involved with a more avant-garde scene in London all demonstrate that Edith is living a life quite different from that of her grandmother. She doesn't find it easy; given the choice, Edith would have happily settled for an utterly conventional life, running a large country house, with two or three children, and doing charity work. But she rises to the challenge of forging a different path for herself and, much to her surprise, finds that she enjoys it.

Many women found that, without marriage as an option, they were liberated to do other things that might not have otherwise been possible, whether it was studying for a degree, running their own business or simply going out to work. It was these women and their pioneering attitude that began to change the cultural and social fabric in terms of how the fairer sex was viewed, paving the way for gender equality several decades later. Edith is one of these women, although she hardly knows it. How brave she really is, is yet to be truly tested.

Anna Robbins, the costume designer of series five, reflects Edith's point of difference in her wardrobe: 'In series four she was dressed in primary blocks of greens, oranges and peaches. We've followed on from that [in series five] and kept her look very positive. I always like to have a coat that represents a character, so we've given her a cashmere turquoise coat with a funnel. I think Edith's really found herself and she's become beautiful. Yet she's more internalised than the others. Also, now she's not in London so much, we can't do as many of the avant-garde looks – she has to dip down and come back up again in terms of having an edge to her style.'

Laura's been enjoying the clothes too: 'They're beautiful – there's a velvet dress which is stunning. Everything feels more modern and the hemlines are still coming up. Edith's been wearing more practical clothes for this series, as she's going down to the farm and is outdoors a lot. But she's got style.'

HOW TO DRIVE

FROM THE BOOK OF ETIQUETTE
BY LADY TROUBRIDGE
(PUBLISHED IN 1926)

There is very definite etiquette in motoring. First, there are the rules which the driver of the car should follow... An uncourteous and unkind habit is to sound the horn wildly and for no other reason than to frighten less fortunate people who have to walk... Another point too often ignored by motorists is to dash at high speed through muddy streets, entirely regardless whether passers-by are bespattered or not. Considerate motorists, in passing through villages in hot weather, will slow down in order to raise as little dust as possible. Inconsiderate ones drive through with no slackening of speed, leaving a whirlwind of dust behind them to find its way into shops and houses.

The people inside the car also have some rules of good conduct to observe. It is bad form to stand up in the car, to sing or shout or make oneself conspicuous; and equally bad form to throw paper bags, used sandwich boxes, or anything else from the car on to the road.

WHITE STAR LINE
THE WORLD'S LARGEST LINER
SOUTHAMPTON
CHERBOURG
NEW YORK

One place where chic flourished in abundance was at sea. The advent of vast ocean liners in 1870, with first-class cabins, electricity and running water, changed long-distance travel significantly. One no longer had to be a sailor, pirate or stowaway to travel the seven seas, as you could now journey between America and England in a manner to which the rich were accustomed on land. Even the poor-but-hopeful were able to cross the oceans as far as Australia in search of a new life, although they were not privy to the comforts of the casino, dining room and elaborate dances that took place on the upper decks.

Nor was it just the working classes that used ocean liners to improve their lives – they were a helpful step on the social ladder for the upper-middle classes, too. Lady Troubridge's strict book of etiquette states that 'the rule of social etiquette… is relaxed on board ship to the extent of permitting the passengers to talk to one another'.

'If she [Rosamund] wishes to be understood by a foreigner, she shouts.'
VIOLET

Julian explains that this was part of the attraction of travelling on cruise ships: 'It was somehow easier to fudge one's own background. The great appeal of cruise ships – like the appeal of Empire – was that when you went to these far-flung places, the rules were relaxed. Not abolished altogether, but you could get into relationships that would have been more difficult back home. In the colonial outposts it was possible to achieve a level of greatness that couldn't be matched back home if you only had your pension to live off. Those cruise ships brought possibilities, like the 'fishing fleets' of India [when English women sought husbands in the Raj if they couldn't find one at home]. My aunts Isie and Ierne, however, went on the fishing fleets and returned empty-handed!'

With the sumptuousness awaiting them on the ships, it was only right that the rich should travel in style. Mrs Wichfeld, a rich American living at Blair Castle in the early 1920s, was remembered by her husband's former valet as one who travelled in a regal state, taking with her seven or eight trunks and some twenty-nine pieces of hand-luggage: 'All these trunks were specially built, with or without drawers. One contained nothing but her stationery, several contained underclothes only. There were special shoe trunks, fitted with trays, each tray sub-divided into baize-lined compartments. First the shoes were put into matching bags, black in black, brown in brown, whatever the colour of the shoe it had a corresponding bag made of moiré silk and lined with a fine chamois leather, and these, of course, were further divided into day shoes, evening shoes, town and country shoes.' For the jewellery, 'some of the Vuitton trunks contained safes and there was one bag which, on trains, never left her Belgian maid's hand'.

CREAM OF WATERCRESS SOUP

Watercress grows all over the British Isles in streams and wet soil – but even in the 1920s it was being grown commercially to meet demand. Sorrel or spinach may be used if watercress isn't available.

SERVES 4

50g butter
1 large onion, peeled
   and chopped
1 large leek (white part
   only), washed and sliced
1 large potato, peeled
   and chopped
salt and pepper
750ml hot chicken stock
   or water
300g watercress,
   de-stalked and chopped
a large pinch of freshly
   grated nutmeg
150ml single cream

Melt the butter in a heavy-based saucepan, then add the onion, leek and potato and stir to coat them in the butter. Season with salt and pepper, and let the vegetables sweat with the lid on over a low heat for about 10 minutes, stirring occasionally. When the vegetables are tender, add the hot stock or water. Bring to the boil, then add the watercress and cook for a further 5 minutes. Season with salt, pepper and nutmeg. Take the pan off the heat and liquidise the soup. Stir in the cream and pour into bowls to serve.

SOLE DUGLERE

Sole was a popular choice on hotel menus: this recipe is adapted from the dish that the French chef Adolphe Duglére invented for the Rothschilds in the nineteenth century. Serve with crusty bread or new potatoes and a green salad.

SERVES 2

2 Dover soles, lemon soles
   or plaice, skinned and
   filleted
salt and pepper
2 tomatoes
25g butter
1 small onion,
   finely chopped
2 tablespoons finely chopped
   parsley
1 tablespoon finely chopped
   dill, plus a few fronds for
   garnish
60ml hot fish stock
60ml dry white wine
2 tablespoons double cream

Rinse the fillets and pat dry. Season well with salt and pepper. Roll the fillets into loose parcels.

Put the tomatoes in a small bowl and cover with boiling water. After a couple of minutes, remove them with a spoon and place on a board. When cool enought to handle, peel the skins off and scoop out the seeds, discarding both. Finely chop the flesh and set aside.

Melt the butter in a wide, shallow pan. Add the onion and cook gently until softened – about 10 minutes. Add the chopped tomatoes, parsley and dill. Season and cook for a few more minutes, then place the fillet parcels on top of the mixture. Pour the stock and white wine over them. Cover the pan and simmer for 8–10 minutes until the fish is cooked.

Remove the fillets to serving plates and keep warm. Add the cream to the mixture in the pan and stir well to incorporate, cooking over a gentle heat for a few more minutes. Spoon this sauce over the fillets and garnish with dill to serve.

Valets and lady's maids were considered essential for such trips and were expected to know everything that would be needed on a journey without being told, whether it was to dress the master or mistress for a funeral or fancy-dress ball. 'He must never be caught napping,' wrote Ernest King in *The Green Baize Door*, a memoir of his butler years, 'he must be able to produce everything, even shoes so well polished they may be used as a mirror in an emergency!'

The sinking of the *Titanic* in 1912 – the iconic moment in history which opened the very first episode of *Downton Abbey* – was not the greatest advert for cruise travel, but it seemed not to stem the flow too greatly; besides, for many more years, there were no other options if you wanted to leave Britain.

Until aeroplanes. The first flight by an aeroplane – twelve seconds long – was achieved in 1903 by the Wright brothers; by the time of the First World War, aeroplanes were in force as machines of combat. By 1919, passengers could fly from London to Paris and just five years later, in 1924, Imperial Airways had begun. One of the world's first commercial airlines, it served the British Empire routes to South Africa, India, Malaya and Hong Kong, as well as Europe. Passports, too, were a new introduction, changing the way people travelled. The first travel document, introduced in 1914, was a piece of folded paper covered with a card, describing the passenger's distinguishing features ('Nose: Large. Moustache.'), with photograph and signature. By 1920, following an agreement with the League of Nations, something similar to the standardised passport book we know today had been brought in.

VIOLET: *'I know I'm late, but it couldn't be helped. Cora insisted I come without a maid, but I can't believe she understood the implications.'*

ISOBEL: *'Which are?'*

VIOLET: *'How do I get the guard to take my luggage? And when we arrive in London, what happens then?'*

ISOBEL: *'Fear not. I have never travelled with a maid, and so we can share my knowledge of the jungle.'*

It's no surprise that Hollywood had a boom time in this period – there were new heroes and heroines in town and they weren't the soldiers or aristos of old; they were pilots, movie stars and explorers. Cinema brought the masses closer to these stars, with the aid of magazines and the radio.

DAISY: *'I like the idea of a wireless. To hear people talking and singing in London and all sorts.'*

MOLESLEY: *'What's so good about that, when you can go to the music hall in York? I'd rather hear a live singer, me.'*

The radio, known as 'the wireless' (so-called because they ran off huge batteries before the National Grid came in), was a brand-new contraption that some found exciting, others found bewildering and still others found frightening. Just as the internet has made our world smaller in bringing news and images from across the globe on to tiny screens held in our hand, so the radio brought famous personalities, politicians, even royalty, into the homes of the ordinary man and woman as never before.

On 23 April 1924 King George V and his son, Prince Edward, opened the British Empire Exhibition and made the first royal radio broadcast. Over ten million tuned in and many events were suspended in order that people could listen in. The excitement for every subject of being able to hear their king speak was very real and it was the first tangible moment when the high barriers erected around the royal family started to come down. For some, this signalled a bright future. For others, it could only mean chaos, the total breakdown of everything that had held their world secure.

The wireless arrives at Downton
for the first radio broadcast by King George V.

JULIAN FELLOWES

WRITER & EXECUTIVE PRODUCER

Julian Fellowes, creator, writer and executive producer of *Downton Abbey*, is also The Lord Fellowes of West Stafford, after having been created a life peer in 2011. So we meet for lunch, appropriately enough, at the House of Lords, where a man in white tie signs me in before Julian walks me through the Princes' Chamber to the Peers' Guests' Bar. The ambience is perfect for a *Downton Abbey* meeting. It is not our first lunch together – Julian is my uncle, my father's younger brother, and we have always been good luncheon companions. When I was a girl on the cusp of adulthood, I would request that Julian took me out for grown-up lunches in smart Chelsea restaurants, which he dutifully would – he was just the right sort of uncle for the occasion.

We have both always shared an interest in history – that is, the stories of history, some of which came from our family, some from iconic figures of the past, some of which were simply illustrative tales of the human condition. It's probably as true to say that our shared hobby is people, whomever they are and whenever they lived. As we always have, we start by exchanging news and gossip of our many relations and mutual friends. We catch up on what the other is doing, although Julian has always been remarkably prolific and it's all I can do to keep on top of what is happening during any given week, let alone the year. It is testament to *Downton Abbey* that while the first ever series was being made, it was the only project that Julian referred to more than once as something he was rather excited about; it was the first tiny inkling I had that this might be A Big Deal. Of course, we weren't to know how much. 'I do find the phenomenon of *Downton* extraordinary,' says Julian. 'We are now officially the most successful television programme this country has ever produced and you wouldn't dare to dream of that.'

Charford Manor, pictured here, was the home of Julian's great-grandfather, John Wrightson.
He was President of Downton Agricultural College, hence the name of the show.
Most of the original house has sadly since been pulled down.

As to why it has been so successful, Julian thinks this comes down to the fact that 'we're basically watching a bunch of fairly decent characters – even Thomas has some decency in him – and I think audiences enjoy that because we're a bit worn out watching those we don't like'. It is this very likeability that has led to what Julian calls 'the Classic *Downton* Conundrum', which is when the audience doesn't always know whose side to take. In every *Downton* dilemma, both sides of the fence are not only visible but easily sat on. Nor does Julian believe that villainy is the only dramatically interesting character trait to explore; in the case of Anna, for example, 'the rape story was very important to me, and the involvement of Anna was key. All my life, I have witnessed the culture that implies the victim must accept some level of blame. I disagree with this absolutely, and I wanted a story where there could be no question of shared guilt. By making Anna the victim, we ensured that. As a matter of fact, I have received letters since from abused women who felt they had been blamed, at least in part, and the *Downton* story had helped them, which I am extremely glad of.'

The show is propelled by the characters and this is an important distinction in Julian's writing. 'It's an actors' show, in that it's driven by the characters' narratives as opposed to some incredibly complicated plotline where the hero has to get to the bomb before the clock strikes twelve.' Nevertheless, with myriad characters in the show, there are a lot of plates to keep spinning. All of the stories are given equal weight and this is key – 'it means you are never going to the lesser story, you're just going to *this* story'.

Before Julian starts writing a series, he has a crib sheet on which he has all of the historical events for that period. The very big over-arching plotlines – for example, Anna's attack and the effects on her marriage – are discussed between Julian, Gareth and Liz, before he goes away and writes the first draft. That draft is read by his wife,

Emma, who has always had sight of everything Julian writes before anyone else; she makes notes, which he works through before handing it on. Gareth and Liz then read it and Gareth synthesises their notes – 'there are a lot of notes at this point, and I take most of them in.' A second draft, another round of notes and then it goes to ITV, who will make some notes of their own. After that, the script editor has it and once it's a shooting script, changes are relatively minor and usually to do with props, 'if something can't be got hold of or a location won't work or whatever,' he explains.

And what of the language the characters use? English, of course, but is it specifically of its time? 'You have to be careful – you can't use too much of the slang from the period, as it would alienate the audience, though I drop in a bit now and then. [Such as when Rose says she is 'puffed' to see someone, meaning pleased.] But I do deliberately put in modern-sounding language, partly to relax the audience by using parlance they are familiar with. But I always check that it was in use at that time.' It's good to be reminded, I say, that we did not invent everything in the twenty-first century, and Julian nods.

Julian is fond of his characters and their fundamental decency, but it is the era they are in that is the source of the show's central theme of change and of compelling interest to their creator. It was, in many ways, an apocalyptic time, with European monarchies falling and the aristocracy feeling under attack by new socialist governments. 'Why should they believe it was anything other than the end?' he says. 'If you lived then, the temptation would be to think, "It's all going to be over by 1930, let's enjoy it while it lasts."'

Writing the show seems to come entirely naturally to Julian – though one shouldn't underestimate the technical skill that makes it appear that way – and there is definitely some truth in the idea, as Gareth Neame spotted in his original outline, that Julian had lived with the characters for a long time before he wrote them on to the page.

As a young man growing up in the 1960s, another period when the last embers of upper-class life were being stamped out, Julian would seek out older relatives in order to hear their stories about what their youth had been like. It was his closeness to his aunt, Isie, his grandfather's sister, that later provided the inspiration, as well as some actual lines, including 'What is a weekend?' for Violet, the Dowager Countess, and the wonderful quip about bought marmalade being 'very feeble' for Lady Trentham in Gosford Park, both played by the impeccable Maggie Smith. If the world of Downton Abbey feels real, it's because, once, it was.

Julian is the youngest of four brothers (from left to right): Rory, Julian, Nicholas and David.

MAY
Debutantes

MAY

There was one event in the lives of young upper-class girls in the early 1920s that was anticipated for many months with feverish excitement. It signified their overnight transformation from child to young woman — the moment, in short, when they exited the schoolroom and entered the ballroom.

ot their wedding, but their presentation at court, marking them out as a debutante for the London Season. For Lady Rose MacClare, cousin of Robert and the charge of the Granthams while her parents are abroad, it is a chance to buy new dresses, make new friends and, hopefully, pick up a handsome suitor or two.

The tradition of introducing men and women to the monarch by way of validating their aristocratic status had been going on since Elizabeth I, but the debutante season took on its formal shape under King George III (1760–1820), when young girls were first recorded as being presented during his wife Queen Charlotte's birthday ball. The ball itself died when the King did and was only revived in 1925 as a charitable event (and led to the myth of debs curtseying to a giant birthday cake – in fact, they curtseyed to the president of the ball, who stood beside the cake). But the ritual of introducing young women to the monarch as a way of launching their debut in society (and again on their marriage, so you were effectively presented twice) continued. Under Queen Victoria, the debutantes would even receive a Certificate of Presentation, providing sure evidence of their credentials.

Having had a hiatus during the First World War, the debutante season proper had only returned the year before Rose's coming out. There had been no court presentations at all between 1915 and 1919, and then there were so many applicants that they were done in the gardens of Buckingham Palace, a great disappointment to many, who would have preferred the splendour of being inside the throne room. They were only felt to have returned to 'normal' in 1922, so for Rose, coming out a year later, the event enjoyed something of the glamour of novelty as well as of tradition. Rose is, says Julian, 'a child of the new world – she doesn't really remember a time before the war'. This means that Rose likes to do things differently; she is less captivated by tradition and revels in opportunities to

Debutantes preparing to be presented to Queen Victoria.

shock the older generations, particularly her mother. But in some respects, she is happy to conform to the expectations of her family and class; when it comes to the aristocratic system for sending its people onwards, she boards its train.

'I suppose it came to me that these balls and presentations and comings out are not just aristocratic fol-de-rol, but traditions by which the members of this family measure their progress through life.'

ISOBEL

In the two hundred years or so since court presentations had formally taken place – and more informally for another two hundred years before that – little had changed. Violet and Cora, both presented to Queen Victoria, would have had almost exactly the same experience. Cora's season took place in 1890 – 'I'd only been in the schoolroom a few months before,' she says, 'but my mother was eager.' Martha Levinson, who had brought Cora to London in 1890, would have been keen to take advantage of the marriageable prospects of a young debutante in London, so that she could marry her daughter's money to a titled family, and in this she was quite tenacious. A great many American mothers felt the same way and achieved the same success – between 1870 and 1914, there were more than one hundred marriages of British peers' sons to young, moneyed American daughters.

In many ways, it was easier to enter into high society in England than in America. An application would be made to the Lord Chamberlain's office at St James's Palace often by the young girl's mother but equally could be anyone else, so long as she had been presented herself at least three years before – and, if approved, she would receive her magic ticket: a presentation card. If you could find an impoverished peeress who had been presented herself, she could be persuaded, for a few pounds, to do the same for your daughter.

With this firmly in hand, preparations for the day could begin, sometimes several months before. Magazines – *The Girl's Realm, The Queen, The Lady* – ran articles in the weeks running up to May and June (when court presentations took place), advising the debs and their mothers on what to expect, how to behave and, crucially, what was needed for their wardrobe.

There were royal guidelines on this, issued by the palace's own favourite dressmakers, Reville Ltd. Under Queen Victoria, the young women were instructed to wear three plumes of ostrich feathers in their hair (representing the Prince of Wales), two yards of tulle or lace falling down the back of the hair and a four foot-long train. The dress itself, which was always white, had to be low in the bodice and short-sleeved, with long white gloves, unless one was in mourning, in which case black or lavender gloves were acceptable.

Left: Advertisement for Reville Ltd, the approved dressmakers for court presentations.

Below: Cora and Rose.

After the First World War, the feathers remained in place, despite the fact that they were quite hard to fix to bobbed hair, but the train was shortened to '18 inches from the heel'. This was probably done partly as a nod to post-war economy, but largely because it sped up the curtseying debs. Having to gather up an enormous train, usually with the help of a courtier standing by, and sidle backwards away from the monarch, was, understandably, both slow and tricky to do. The dress itself, after the war, did not have to be floor-length (or pure white) and Rose is seen taking full advantage of this to wear a dress that was, in shape, only fashionable for a brief few months in 1923, with a shorter skirt and extra-wide hips.

'Of course, a single peer with a good estate won't be lonely long if he doesn't want to be.'

LADY SHACKLETON

No make-up would be worn, except perhaps a tiny bit of powder to stop shiny noses and rosebud-coloured lipsalve, although they might have had a manicure, 'so a girl could look groomed rather than wanton', explains the social historian Lucinda Gosling in her book *Debutantes and the London Season*. Rose might, however, have splashed on a bit of scent. Expert Lizzie Ostrom says she would have 'made a beeline for the ultimate flapper fragrance purveyors, Caron, whose 1922 release Nuit de Noël came in a black flask-shaped bottle with a band round the rim designed to look like the headgear of a Bright Young Thing. It had a mossy, heady scent, garlanded with deep roses.'

There were just three or four court presentations in the year, with one specially devoted to ladies connected to the diplomatic service. Under Queen Victoria, the presentations took place from three o'clock in the afternoon and lasted several hours, with no refreshments available for the wilting debs, nor even a loo – just a chamber pot behind a screen. King Edward VII – always a man who liked a good party – moved the presentations to the evening, where they stayed.

The number of requests, there could be hundreds, meant there would be an enormous and slow queue building up outside the palace. Debs were eager to be one of the first in the room, as it was not unheard of for the monarch to tire of the event and pass the baton to one of their less glamorous relatives. It was also far more fun to hang around in the throne room after being presented to watch the other girls – there was bound to be at least one misjudged curtsey to provide amusement.

Before the women and their sponsors even got to Buckingham Palace, they would spend a few hours sitting in a long line of cars down the Mall – that marvellous route laid out for processions between Admiralty Arch (leading to Trafalgar Square) and the enormous black iron gates of the palace. Crowds would gather to watch the debs, with newsreel crews and press photographers among them. In 1927 *Bystander* reported that some from the throng even stood on the footboards of the cars to get a better view: 'More venturesome souls, apparently thinking this waiting is for their especial benefit, actually open the doors.'

Once the debs and their sponsors had assembled in the presence chamber, an ante-room to the throne room, they would nervously wait their turn. At the signal to go in, the girl would enter with her sponsor and hand her presentation card to the Lord Chamberlain. As former deb Loelia Ponsonby recalls, it was '… over in a flash. One reached the head of the queue, handed one's invitation to a splendid official, he shouted aloud one's name and tossed the card into a rather common-looking little wastepaper basket, one advanced along the red carpet, stopped and made two curtsies to the King and Queen who were sitting on a low dais surrounded by numerous relations and then walked on.'

Loelia was presented to King George V and Queen Mary, as was Rose. The Queen was a popular figure in her day, having led by example in encouraging much of the women's war effort by being seen to visit the wounded and dying soldiers and leading a drive to send parcels to those at the front – all conducted with a perfectly stiff-upper-lip manner, even as tragedy raged all around.

King George V and Queen Mary with the Prince of Wales and the Princess Royal standing beside them.

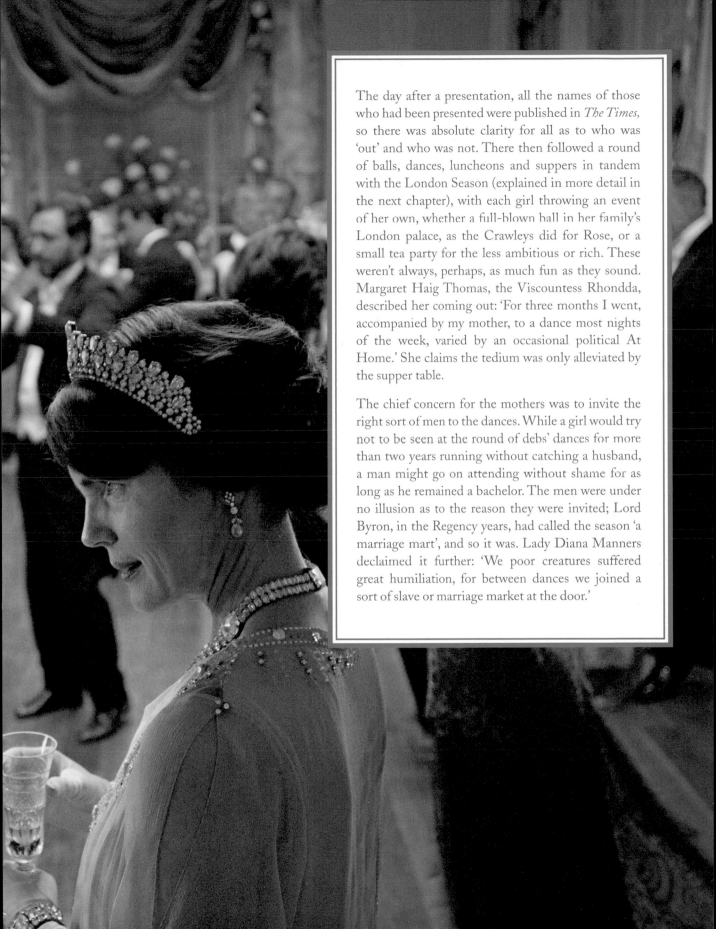

The day after a presentation, all the names of those who had been presented were published in *The Times*, so there was absolute clarity for all as to who was 'out' and who was not. There then followed a round of balls, dances, luncheons and suppers in tandem with the London Season (explained in more detail in the next chapter), with each girl throwing an event of her own, whether a full-blown ball in her family's London palace, as the Crawleys did for Rose, or a small tea party for the less ambitious or rich. These weren't always, perhaps, as much fun as they sound. Margaret Haig Thomas, the Viscountess Rhondda, described her coming out: 'For three months I went, accompanied by my mother, to a dance most nights of the week, varied by an occasional political At Home.' She claims the tedium was only alleviated by the supper table.

The chief concern for the mothers was to invite the right sort of men to the dances. While a girl would try not to be seen at the round of debs' dances for more than two years running without catching a husband, a man might go on attending without shame for as long as he remained a bachelor. The men were under no illusion as to the reason they were invited; Lord Byron, in the Regency years, had called the season 'a marriage mart', and so it was. Lady Diana Manners declaimed it further: 'We poor creatures suffered great humiliation, for between dances we joined a sort of slave or marriage market at the door.'

ASPARAGUS TART

English asparagus is unparalleled in flavour – use the freshest you can find to make this tart, which is perfect for a starter or light lunch. If you prefer, you can make several smaller tartlets.

SERVES 4

175g plain flour, plus extra
    for dusting
salt and pepper
75g butter
2–3 tablespoons iced water
a bunch of asparagus
4 eggs
300ml single cream
40g Parmesan, finely grated
a pinch of freshly grated
    nutmeg
a few sprigs of thyme,
    leaves picked

Preheat the oven to 180°C/350°F/gas 4.

Sieve the flour into a mixing bowl with a large pinch of salt. Crumble in the butter and rub into the flour to give crumb texture. Add the iced water, one tablespoon at a time – just enough to bring the mixture into a ball of dough with your hands.

Dust the worktop and a rolling pin with flour. Roll the dough out thinly into a circle that is large enough to fill a 20cm tart tin or dish. Carefully lift the dough circle into place and press it into the tin. Trim the edges with a knife. Prick the base all over with a fork, fill with baking beans and bake in the oven for 20 minutes.

Snap off the hard parts at the end of the asparagus, and trim the ends with a knife to neaten. Wash the spears well and place in a pot of water that will hold them horizontally. Bring to the boil, simmer for a few minutes until half cooked and drain.

Remove the tart from the oven, remove the baking beans and return the pastry to the oven for a further 5 minutes. Leave the pastry case to one side while you prepare the filling.

Beat the eggs in a mixing bowl. Stir in the cream and then the Parmesan until well combined. Season with salt, pepper and nutmeg.

Dry the asparagus spears with kitchen paper. Arrange them in a fan in the bottom of the pastry case. Carefully pour the egg mixture around the asparagus until the tart case is almost full. Sprinkle the thyme leaves over the top. Bake in the oven for about 40 minutes, until golden.

Serve the tart hot, cut into wedges, with a green salad.

Lady Rose with Mrs Dudley Ward, a well-known mistress of the Prince of Wales.

The women of the 1920s seem to have been rather dismissive of the available men. Mary Clive, the daughter of an Irish earl, wrote in her memoir, *Brought Up and Brought Out:* 'It was of course considered very vulgar for a man to dance well (like talking French at school with a French accent) and, if by any chance one did meet a man who did it beautifully, one was absolutely safe in writing him off as a bounder.' Mothers and chaperones passed between each other the list of 'deb's delights', those young men who could be relied upon to make up the numbers and behave themselves. In later years, the list included those who were not to be invited unless absolutely desperate – they might be marked as NSIT ('not safe in taxis') or MTF ('must touch flesh'). Lucinda Gosling writes that if the numbers were really short, notices alerting male students to forthcoming debutante balls would be pinned up in the medical and law faculties of universities. The students would be sure to come, if only for the free food and drink (some things never change).

The difficulty for many of the girls was that despite the fact that the intention was to find a husband, it was nigh on impossible for anything romantic to happen under the beady eyes of the mothers and chaperones sitting round the edges of the dances. The actress Joyce Grenfell wrote that even in 1928, if her parents were not also going to a dance she had been invited to, she would be escorted by the family maid.

Why were the women so keen to collude with this set-up? Largely because, for the upper-class young girl, marriage was her escape route out of the family home; her means of independence and the chance to build a power base of her own. Choosing a husband from the men presented to her during the balls and parties of the season meant she was more likely to fall in love with 'the right sort' than not. It wasn't that marriages were arranged so much as it was hoped that if you put your daughter in the right circles, you stood a better chance of gaining a son-in-law with a title and money. But whereas upper-class girls before the First World War were very sheltered from boys before they came out and were likely to marry the first man they kissed, by the 1920s, spending time together was miles easier. It was becoming more accepted that a girl might pick and choose whom she liked and maybe even spend time with a possible suitor before making a decision But even this level of daring did not go much beyond the holding of hands and a stolen kiss or two.

MARY: 'The older I get, the more I feel we do these things very oddly. Even now we must decide whether to share our lives with someone without spending any real time with them. Let alone… you know.'

MARY: *'Obviously it's very shocking to to someone of your generation.'*

VIOLET: *'Don't let's hide behind the changing times, my dear. This is shocking to most people in 1924.'*

Mary's reputation, of course, almost foundered to the point of rendering her unmarriageable after she succumbed to a seduction by the devastatingly handsome Kemal Pamuk that ended tragically (he died in her bed, in the first series). Perhaps she didn't really understand what she was letting herself in for when she admitted him into her bedroom; perhaps she thought she could keep it a secret. She wouldn't have been the first – it is based on a true story, told to Julian years before he even thought of *Downton Abbey* – and it was bad luck that it ended the way it did. But although men and women of the world would have known such things went on (that is, sexual relations outside of marriage), they would have found it profoundly shocking in an earl's unmarried daughter.

Remarkably, it was almost entirely the opposite for the working classes. When the governess, Lettuce [*sic*], confesses to the nanny, Emily, in *Tea by the Nursery Fire*, that she is illegitimate, the nanny's biographer writes: 'Emily thought nothing of that. In Easden [the village where she grew up] any girl who walked out regularly with a boy took it for granted he would only marry her last minute. No bride ever reached the altar without obviously carrying her groom's baby.' Confirming this view is Edwin Lee, the butler at Cliveden, who came from a farming family and remembered that no man would risk a barren wife. He tells the tale of two village women gossiping sometime in the late nineteenth century.

'I hear Hilda Brown is getting married.'
'Is she? I didn't know she was pregnant.'
'She isn't, bloody snob.'

Cora and Lady Rose ascend the stairs to the throne room.

Creating the episode for Rose's coming out was no mean feat. Lancaster House in London was chosen as the location for Buckingham Palace. It was once London's most expensive private house, with an interior that set the fashion for the city's smartest drawing rooms: Queen Victoria was alleged to have said to the Duchess of Sutherland, 'I have come from my house to your palace.' It is now a government building, occasionally used for receptions and largely closed to the public.

From the cast, only Elizabeth McGovern (Cora), Lily James (Lady Rose) and Hugh Bonneville (Robert) were present, as they would have been the only family members there in the throne room. There were also the actors Oliver Dimsdale and Guy Williams, as the Prince of Wales and King George respectively, the two other speaking parts for that scene. Queen Mary was played by the third assistant director's mother, as she happens to bear a strong resemblance! Alastair Bruce was given the part of the Lord Chamberlain; he was the man who not only handled all the debutante applications, but then read out their names to announce them to the King and Queen. 'I was rather keen on giving myself the Order of the Garter,' laughs Alastair. 'It hadn't actually been given to the Lord Chamberlain until 1924, so I brought that in a little earlier!'

Alastair was involved in the research into exactly what would have happened during the court presentation: 'Getting uniform insignia and court dress right was the biggest challenge because people may write that they attended an event but not say exactly what they wore. We realised only at the last minute that I was about to be dressed in the wrong trousers and jacket. There is a difference between the court dress — which is worn in the evening — of privy councillors, which is red collar and red cuffs, and the royal household, which is gold collar and gold cuffs. So we had to find more gold collars and cuffs.' Alastair did much of his research digging deep in the archives of Windsor Castle, examining the court papers and trying to find the documents of the Master of the Household that might tell him the format of the presentation.

HOW TO CURTSEY AT COURT

Young ladies preparing for their debutante season would almost invariably be sent to Madame Vacani's School of Dance to learn the deep court curtsey. To achieve this, you glide forward, keeping your eyes fixed upon the monarch all the while. Put your left foot a little forward and lean your weight upon it, sliding your right foot behind, on tiptoes. Those being presented would hold a small posy in front while sinking down as low as possible – the grander you are, the maxim goes, the lower you go – with back and neck absolutely straight. (On other occasions, dip down with your arms by your sides.) Smile the whole while, keeping your eyes on the royal personage, bowing your head just before rising. If you have curtsied to the King, you must then discreetly kick your long skirt out of the way, take three steps to the right and repeat the curtsey to the Queen. Finally, walk backwards away from the monarch – you must never turn your back. Courtiers may be on hand to help with your train.

As well as the cast, an enormous number of extras were needed for this episode. The call-sheet for the day is illuminating: 6 x presenting ladies; 10 x debutantes; 1 x Yeoman of the Guard; 3 x palace footmen; 3 x gentlemen users; Fierce Aunt; 3 x household officers… and so on. Each one would be in costume early – Caroline McCall, the costume designer for series four, and her team had to be on set by 5 a.m. to prepare. 'We had at least twelve extra helpers on the day to dress the crowd,' she says. To gather the costumes, they found as many cream and white dresses as they could, largely from the hire house Cosprop, and then made simple trains. 'There were so many regulations in terms of how many inches on the floor, and we wanted to get it as correct as we possibly could, so that did take time. My assistant had to make sure everything to do with medals was correct and that was tough! Afterwards we wondered how we did it, but the more you have to do, the more you achieve. We were running on adrenaline.'

Of course, the star of the show was Rose. 'Her style was very of the moment and when you look at the images you can't quite believe that that moment is 1923,' says Caroline. 'There were so many different designs happening then, dropping in and out. I had two ideas for Rose's coming out and chose three styles to show Liz Trubridge and Julian. I said we could either go for something very beaded and quite shocking, to show what a rebel she is – I thought she might choose something that would upset her mother with a picture of her wearing it in the paper – or something much more romantic, with roses and embroidery. Julian felt that Rose would conform for the occasion and he liked the idea for the prettier dress.' For Rose's own ball in the evening, the director wanted her to wear a strong colour rather than the white she would wear for the presentation. 'So we chose a pink dress in a similar style,' says Caroline. 'When you see her in it – everyone else there is in gold and silver – it means there's no question: it's *her* ball.

Lady Rose's official coming-out ball, where she had the honour of the Prince of Wales asking her for the first dance.

HAIR & MAKE-UP

Nic Collins, hair and make-up designer, joined *Downton Abbey* for the fifth series. A fan of the show, she admits she found coming on to the set for the first time very exciting, but also quite frightening.

Nic's work began in early January: 'We have four weeks' prep and at the beginning we had meetings to establish whether we would be maintaining the looks of previous series or if there was movement for change with the characters. I also would say where I felt we could enhance or alter. Hair and make-up helps create a character; I wanted to widen the gap between the looks above and below stairs.'

Nic and I are talking in the hair and make-up truck – it is packed with a sweet shop of delights, from luxurious skincare products to lipstick palettes. One side of the truck is lined with six huge mirrors, framed with bright strip lights (presumably more practical than the pretty dressing-room light-bulb frames of old) and six chairs; along the back is a shelf with several faceless polystyrene busts wearing various wigs. 'Nearly everybody has some kind of wig, piece or switch [smaller clips of hair to add length or volume],' says Nic.

Lily James receives a finishing touch.

This is partly down to the time factor – there's a huge cast to be got ready every morning, so they cannot spend more than an hour and fifteen minutes on each female character, and putting a wig on is a lot quicker than doing their curls. Even the male actors need twenty to thirty minutes each: 'It depends on the haircuts – the men must have one every week to keep them exactly the same.' As well as the main cast, there will be 'crowd' actors to be prepared daily – from hall boys and maids in the kitchen to fellow guests at a London party. Nic has a permanent team of six and 'endless amounts of daily help, sometimes as many as twenty freelance make-up artists. We need manpower.'

The year 1924 was a very exciting one for hair and make-up. It was the year of the shingle bob: a short, chin-length bob that goes up at the nape of the neck and drops down at the side. That year, half of all women in Britain had their hair bobbed. Before then, girls wore their hair down as children, and putting it up was a mark of reaching womanhood. Cutting your hair into a bob was still a very daring thing to do in the early post-war years, and many, as with Edith and Mary, chose instead to ape the style by shaping the front sections of their hair into a bob and pinning up the long hair at the back of their necks. In

1924, the bob became an expression of independence and was a fiery topic of debate – sometimes more, with divorce and murder allegedly attributed to the emotions stirred by the simple haircut.

Even if you chose not to bob your hair, there was a definite focus on styling and accessories. From tortoiseshell combs to scarves and turbans, women liked to pay attention to their heads. And, of course, there were the waves. Initially, women used the Marcel tongs. Nic has some in her truck and they resemble scissors with long, thin tongs; these would be heated in a little oven before being wound round the hair. But the curls achieved are rather angular and Nic wanted to move into a softer, more rounded look, which was becoming increasingly fashionable as the 1920s moved on. Now, as then, Nic's team do finger waves, a styling method which uses just gel and water (the hair is 'pinched' into S-curls when wet and dries naturally) – it has the benefit of being far less damaging to the actors' hair.

Laura Carmichael, as Lady Edith, has her hair curled in this way for the daytime scenes: 'She wears a wig for the dining scenes,' says Nic, 'the problem being that hats go on and off during the day, ruining the curls.' Michelle Dockery (Lady Mary) and Lily James (Lady Rose) wear wigs all the time and Elizabeth McGovern (Cora) has just a switch for the back. Above stairs, the only actress we see on screen with all her own hair is Daisy Lewis (Sarah Bunting).

Make-up, too, began to be increasingly used, losing its lowly associations with tarts and actresses. The glamour of the new movie stars probably had a great deal to do with this, and many women liked to imitate their smoky eyes and wine-coloured lips. As Downton Abbey does not move as fast as Hollywood, to say the least, Nic cannot paint the cast with too much make-up, but the natural look is being gently updated with some darker lipsticks and a little more eye-shadow than before. 'We're helped by the fact that the 1920s' looks seem to be fashionable again today,' says Nic. 'Lady Mary wears Julie Hewett lipsticks in Sin Noir and Film Noir colours, with gorgeous period-style packaging. Lady Edith uses taupe and brown palettes by Laura Mercier and Bobbi Brown.'

Actresses below stairs have to look completely natural. Nic's team tint their eyebrows and eyelashes, so that no products have to be used there, and then it's just a skin primer followed by a light base (foundation mixed with a little oil and then applied using either a natural sponge or a special airbrush spray gun to give everyone a natural, healthy sheen), with some base and corrector. They are even given lip treatments so they don't get chapped lips.

The men need to look groomed, so they'll have the same light base applied, and any marks and blemishes will be covered, 'Though we're careful not to even out the tone and we'll give them washes of colour,' says Nic.

Each actor and actress has their own make-up bag and their own exclusive products – 'It's about creating individuals rather than generic colours on everybody.' This reflects exactly the approach of the show to its characters and demonstrates how carefully every detail is thought through.

Sophie McShera's natural look and (inset) Lily's wig.

JUNE
The London Season

JUNE

In 1924 there was only one place to be in June if you were fashionable and rich: London. For several decades, this had been the headiest month of 'the season' which began in the first week of May with a Private View at Burlington House, home to the Royal Academy, and lasted until the end of July, with the races at Goodwood as the final event.

In these exhilarating weeks almost every conceivable kind of occasion took place in London, or just outside it, whether sporting, theatrical, floral or plain old party. Kicking off with the Royal Academy's Summer Exhibition, there followed polo at Hurlingham, Roehampton and Ranelagh; racing at Ascot; the All England Tennis Championships at Wimbledon; the Eton–Harrow and Oxford–Cambridge cricket matches; the Fourth of June (a picnic at Eton commemorating a visit made to the school on that date by King George III) and numerous concerts, fêtes, recitals, luncheons, parties and balls. The city was a whirligig of amusements and beautifully dressed men and women. If you were young, good-looking and rich in 1924, the fun was there to be had. (Truth be told, if you are young, good-looking and rich in almost any year, the fun is there to be had. And a great many of those season events still happen today.)

Initially, the season had begun as an amorphous thing, a rather exclusive round of functions for the very grandest families in England, all staying in their London palaces while the men attended Parliament. This 'Little Season' ran during the Parliamentary session from February to July, gradually shortening its calendar to the round of annual events popular in Queen Victoria's reign, which carried on to the twentieth century. Over time it became more of a spectacle, with the nouveau riche, artists, Hollywood stars, musicians and so on all joining in, as well as crowds of spectators lining the route to witness the famous and infamous in their fabulous dresses. The season became almost as much of an event for those not actually taking part as for those in it.

The Crawley family are seen for the first time at their London base – Grantham House – in the fourth series. In keeping with many such families of the time, they keep their London house closed, bar one or two servants permanently living in, unless the family are staying there. For most of the year, for their occasional trips to see their dressmaker or milliner, the daughters and Cora prefer to stay with Rosamund, Robert's sister, to save their staff the bother of opening up the house just for one or two nights. Robert, if up for business (one is always 'up' to London and 'down' to the country, whether your country residence is north, south, east or west of the city), stays either with Rosamund or possibly in his club, most likely White's, one of the older, grander establishments of Pall Mall and St James's.

Of course, those families who went backwards and forwards quite a bit, such as the Astors (whose country house was Cliveden), would keep their London household running on a fully operational basis: in 1928 they had a full-time staff of housekeeper, head housemaid, two under-housemaids, an odd man, a carpenter and an electrician. There was also a controller, who looked after all the households, three accountants and a number of secretaries – as many as seven when Lady Astor was MP (she was the first female MP to sit in the House of Commons).

When the Crawleys go to London for Rose's court presentation and coming-out ball, they take most of their servants with them, although this is partly because Mrs Bute, their London housekeeper, is ill with scarlet fever. A skeletal staff remains behind at Downton to look after Tom Branson. As Julian explains: 'The Crawleys are medium-grand and they don't have the money to waste all year round. So they would only open up the house for the season, but that wasn't unusual.'

While Rose is the chief reason for the family going to London, that's not to say the rest of them don't enjoy the season too. Cora, Mary and Edith especially will use the time to visit dressmakers and fashionable couture houses, as well as catch up with friends and cultural events. While they hold occasional house parties at home, Downton Abbey, being in Yorkshire, is not somewhere many of their friends can visit easily for one supper. In London, they can enjoy both accepting and issuing rather more spontaneous invitations. The best of these are the 'At Home' parties, which begin after dinner has ended, with various people dropping in and a light supper served at 11 p.m. These are a headache for Mrs Patmore – she never knows exactly how many people will turn up, so we see her prepare dishes that could be served to several, such as kedgeree.

*Lady
Rosamund
Painswick*

Rose, in common with her peers, much prefers to end her evenings at a nightclub. These were still a novelty concept in 1924 and were definitely considered rather dubious, with illicit goings-on. Quite a few parents forbade their daughters from going to nightclubs, as one deb complained: 'They did not see any difference between a place like Uncle's where you drank beer in a teacup [in imitation of American prohibition] in case the police called or the Fifty-Three with its squad of girls, and Ciro's and the Embassy which had nothing sinister about them.' Nevertheless, the rebel ignored her parents and went to the Embassy as often as she could: 'It was the favourite meeting place of all my friends and so it was like going to a lovely party where one knew everyone.'

Like his grandfather, the Prince of Wales was a man who enjoyed dressing up, parties and the company of women. The Kit-Cat Club became known as 'virtually a second home for the Prince of Wales', according to Charlotte Breese, author of *Hutch*, her biography of the popular jazz musician. Which was not to say that he was known for being outrageous – the Prince's affair with Wallis Simpson in 1936 was not revealed to the British public until he abdicated over it.

The average Joe was still relatively naive and the newspapers were still cautious, despite the reputation of the period – in print, syphilis was 'a certain disease', rape was 'a certain suggestion' and pregnancy 'a certain condition'. Perhaps parents of the period can be forgiven for worrying about what went on behind the closed doors of a basement nightclub.

Racy young girls were known as flappers – they didn't wear corsets, exposed their legs below the knee and embraced the new dance bands with open arms and jazz-hands. The change was extraordinarily rapid, given that women had not exposed their legs above the ankles since they wore sacks in medieval times. In 1923, the skirts were still quite long and, in fact, they didn't get as short as one expects of a typical twenties dress until 1925, when suddenly the hemline rose all the way to the knees: as James Laver, the 1920s contemporary fashion commentator, put it, 'It seemed to many that the end of the world had come'. The dresses were getting shorter, inch by inch, each year and there was one striking consequence: women suddenly paid attention to shoes, and stockings, which up to that point had always been plain, black and woollen. Now they had stockings of cotton, silk or artificial silk, in all kinds of colours, some with wonderfully elaborate patterns. Flesh-coloured stockings heightened the impression of nudity, which gave further shocks to the moralists.

Nightclubs were just a part of this general mood of rebellion and the extravagant dances a part of them. The Original Dixieland Jazz Band was one of the first to come over from America, holding a three month season at the Hammersmith Palais de Danse in 1919 and introducing hits such as 'I'm Forever Blowing Bubbles' and 'Tiger Rag'; after that, several followed. In *Downton Abbey*, of course, one of these is Jack Ross and his band.

The story of Rose and Jack Ross, says Julian, was based on the real-life black jazz musician Leslie Hutchinson, known as Hutch. (My own mother-in-law danced as a young girl to his band, which is a nice illustration of how close to us this 'period drama' really is.) Originally from Grenada, he had a great many affairs with high-society women in Paris and London, becoming the subject of a major scandal when a young deb became pregnant by him. She was hastily married off to an army officer, but when the baby was born, it was clear he was not the father; sadly, the baby was adopted and the officer sued his bride's parents.

Hutch, always extremely well-dressed and apparently doused in Chanel No5, was a friend of Josephine Baker's, and after playing at parties hosted by the fashionable Daisy Fellowes (a cousin of Julian's), he became part of the Prince of Wales's fast set and a darling of the 'Bright Young Things' (BYTs). This phrase was coined by the newspapers, who breathlessly followed the exploits of a few beautiful, upper-class young men and women – the members changed over the years, but included Cecil Beaton, Stephen Tennant, Elizabeth Ponsonby (cousin of Loelia), the Jungman sisters and Diana Mitford – who, for a while in the mid-1920s, provided plenty of thrilling copy with their flapper clothes, dance crazes, wild costume parties, alleged orgies and treasure hunts, which involved speeding round London to find 'clues' in the middle of the night. Their antics were perfectly satirised by Evelyn Waugh in his novel *Vile Bodies*.

Charlotte Breese writes that the BYTs – a decade younger than Hutch – and particularly the girls, 'found his exoticism and air of international sophistication preferable to the callow gaucheness of their white partners. He had lived a much wider, more exciting life than most of them... He looked spectacular and rode well in Rotten Row [the see-and-be-seen broad avenue in Hyde Park], and, to the delight of spectators, would often scoop up his bowler from the ground at full gallop.' The attraction Rose has for Jack is based on much the same impression – he is dashing and gallant.

Despite this, Hutch experienced racism: 'You have no idea how much colour prejudice there was in London in those days,' he recalled in the 1960s. 'Many times I was asked to go and sing at big parties in grand houses, I had to go in by the servants' entrance. At the time, I just accepted it as the way things were, but it makes me mad as hell now.' Some claim it was not racial so much as class prejudice. Dame Barbara Cartland remembered inviting Hutch to lunch as a friend, but said: '[He], like Ambrose, that bandleader, always knew his place and did not presume on the fact that we were friends. There was a barrier, not because he was black, but because he was a paid performer.'

Jack Ross

CORA: *'I'm sorry to see them go.'*

ROSE: *'Not as sorry as Mary.
What's a group noun for suitors?'*

CORA: *'What do you think? A desire?'*

ROSAMUND: *'A desire of suitors.
Very good.'*

MARY: *'If you're going to talk nonsense,
I have better things to do.'*

Widowed and recovering from the loss of Matthew, Mary is able to enjoy the season again, if only for the clothes and company she keeps. Still young and beautiful, there's no shortage of admirers, a fact that her family are apt to tease her with.

The season, of course, was the perfect time for budding romances. It's not just the birds and the bees that make the most of spring's sunshine. In 1924, men and women may have been less strait-laced than before the war, but the sexual mores of the Edwardians were still hard to shake off, not least while the older generation were around to comment.

It's hard to gauge what a woman of that time knew about sex, as it wasn't a subject they could read about easily in books or even write about in their diaries (unless they were sure to burn them later). There was a little more information than previous generations had enjoyed, thanks to Marie Stopes, a forward-thinking suffragette who much regretted an unhappy marriage (she divorced her first husband on the grounds that their alliance had never been consummated) and wanted things to be different for other women. Her books *Married Love* and *Wise Parenthood*, published in 1918, were worldwide bestsellers for years, as well as being the subject of huge controversy. She intended them as books on birth control for married couples, but they were often referred to as sex manuals, although the language is scientific in tone and hardly erotic. Mrs Hughes certainly feels she's got the measure of Edna, the maid that seduced Tom Branson, when she finds a copy of *Married Love* in her room.

Lady Mary and Lady Rose talking in the London house.

Even Mary may find the changing times hard to resist for long. In many ways a traditionalist, she is nevertheless drawn to the future – even when she feels uncertain how to respond to new dilemmas. Gareth Neame resists naming a favourite character – 'There's not a weak link, I love all of them' – but says of Mary: 'She's central to the figures in the show. Her grandmother knows her day is gone and Mary knows she is like her, but sees that she belongs to a different era. She has to be a moderniser and where Robert is clinging on, Mary is a pragmatist.' This attitude of hers is reflected in her dress. Anna Robbins, costume designer, says of her wardrobe in series five: 'Her palettes have come out of mourning now, but she's going through a process of discovering things about herself and how she wants life to be.' Anna also thinks Mary has an interest in fashion, even if she takes her own view on it: 'She'd follow Chanel, but there's a pared-down classic take on the fashionable. With Mary, it's not about using bolder, fussy prints, or even textured fabrics, it's about cutting techniques. We use a lot of silk and cashmere for her – others might wear devoré, but she would only ever be in plain velvet. We use monochromatic colours in a Chanel way. Mary is the embodiment of the future of Downton Abbey – the dark greens and dark reds of the house are used in her wardrobe, so that she looks as if she belongs in the room.'

Perhaps Mary might have chosen a scent to underline this new, mature period of her life. Expert Lizzie Ostrom suggests she might wear something sophisticated from the Corsican perfume entrepreneur François Coty: 'Coty's fragrances were exquisitely packaged in Lalique bottles and were very expensive indeed, with a sense of discreet luxury. They were also grown-up, adored by the cognoscenti – his Chypre, from 1917, was inspired by the famous fragrance type of the island of Cyprus, full of mosses and woods, and subsequently much imitated. Chypre is long gone, but Mitsouko from Guerlain, originally dating from 1919, is of a similar type, if fruitier, and still available today.'

At the end of the season, it was suddenly as important not to be seen in London as it had been to be seen in it. There was a mass exodus at the end of July, and certainly by the middle of August (the grouse season begins on the 12th), the only people remaining in the capital would have been decidedly unfashionable. The Crawleys will make their exit well in time. The servants will be wrung out and ready to stretch out again after their cramped quarters in Grantham House. Robert will be looking forward to a little peace and quiet, as well as, presumably, a bit of time off from writing large cheques for his wife's dressmaker and milliner. The women will welcome the respite from the dressing up and sideways glances of London's fashion commentators. Rose will miss the whirl of parties, nightclubs and dances; she must concentrate on finding something to do in Yorkshire that will keep her as occupied and fascinated. All of them will dine out on the gossip they've heard, seen and maybe even created for weeks. That, after all, was part of the point of the season – the pure entertainment value. What japes!

POTTED SALMON

Potting in butter would have been Mrs Patmore's way of using up scraps of fish — kippers and shrimps can be given the same treatment. Serve as a starter, supper dish or as part of a picnic.

SERVES 4

200g butter
1 blade of mace
1 bay leaf
550g poached salmon
    or leftover cooked salmon
a pinch of freshly grated
    nutmeg
a pinch of cayenne pepper
1 tablespoon finely chopped
    dill
zest and juice of ½ lemon
salt and black pepper

Place the butter, mace and bay leaf in a small pan over a medium heat and gently heat until the butter starts to bubble. Remove from the heat, cover and leave to one side for about 30 minutes to infuse.

Meanwhile, flake the salmon into a mixing bowl, discarding any skin and bones. Add the grated nutmeg, cayenne, dill, lemon juice and zest, and season generously with salt and pepper. Pour in a splash of the butter and mix well to combine. Divide the salmon mixture between ramekins or small pots, pressing it down until flat.

Pour the rest of the melted butter through a sieve into a jug, leaving the milky liquid (solids) behind in the pan. Pour the clarified butter over the salmon in the ramekins. Cover the ramekins and chill in the fridge for at least 1 hour. Eat within 3–4 days. Take out of the fridge 15 minutes before serving.

Serve the potted salmon with hot, thin toast and lemon wedges.

MERINGUES
WITH RED BERRIES

Meringues and cream are the perfect foil to all the delicious English berries that are in abundance at this time of year. If you are lucky enough to have wild strawberries growing in your garden, they will help to make this pudding look extra dainty.

SERVES 6

3 large egg whites, at room
    temperature
175g caster sugar
selection of berries such as
    strawberries, raspberries
    and redcurrants
double cream, to serve

Preheat the oven to 140°C/275°F/gas 1. Line two large baking sheets with greaseproof paper.

Place the egg whites in a large bowl and have the sugar measured and ready. Whisk the egg whites using an electric mixer until they form soft peaks (at which stage you should be able to upturn the bowl without them sliding out). Add the sugar little by little, whisking after each addition. When all the sugar is added, the meringue should have a thick, glossy texture.

Place tablespoons of the mixture on to the prepared baking sheets, spacing them evenly apart. Bake in the oven for 1 hour, then turn off the oven and leave the meringues to cool completely with the door ajar.

When you are ready to serve, arrange the berries in a bowl with the meringues and a jug of cream alongside.

COSTUME

Anna Mary Scott Robbins is *Downton Abbey*'s costume designer, joining the show for the fifth series. It's lucky she has a calm and authoritative manner because anyone else might have been daunted by the task before them. 'I did know it was going to be a show like no other because not only is it established and popular, but there's massive hype surrounding the costumes particularly. I knew it would be a tough job to step into,' she laughs.

Costume designers are famously one of the hardest workers on set, the first to arrive and the last to leave: 'I wouldn't even tell you the hours I do because I don't like to say them out loud.' Thankfully, Anna doesn't have to do it all alone – she has a team of ten, including the costume supervisor, wardrobe manager, a cutter and two seamstresses in the workroom.

The wardrobe department at Ealing Studios.

Many of the costumes are made by Anna and her department, which, she explains, she likes: 'Personally, I think it gives you more control over the design and it also means that Carnival, the production company, then owns the asset. It's also a much more effective way of working, as it means that whether we're filming at Ealing Studios [where the workroom is based] or on location, we can constantly add to the wardrobe.' One of the difficulties she faces is that there is a finite number of authentic period costumes in the hire houses and at vintage fairs and many are falling apart, as they are now almost a hundred years old. There simply isn't the choice that there used to be.

Anna began working on the show in December 2013, when she received the first scripts. At that point, she started shopping and doing recces for costume ideas, but she didn't have access to the cast until after Christmas. 'You can't fully design something until you can see how it sits on an actor and I'll often have to call for extra time during the schedule. We'll have twenty minutes to dress an actor if they're wearing something established [worn before], but something new will need half an hour, so we can talk it through and tweak anything.'

Anna will speak to the actor about the look they want for their character: 'Overall, it is a balancing act between the aesthetic design of the whole piece and the characterisation of the individual. I always have to have an eye on the bigger picture. I do like to work collaboratively with actors if they are keen to be involved. Some like to be more involved than others in the part that costume plays in their characterisation.'

Each character requires thinking about in terms of what their clothes say about them and, of course, the range of costumes needed per person can be quite wide – the women above stairs need several evening dresses, day dresses, specific occasion outfits (such as for walking or riding) and all the accessories. The shorter hems in the 1920s meant women started to take more notice of their shoes and stockings for the first time and Anna has been finding printed stockings or those with woven detail on the ankle: 'Some of them are really quite risqué. The new focus on the feet definitely reflected a different framework for their morality.'

Clothing, of course, starts next to the skin with underwear. By 1924, most women – excepting the more old-fashioned, such as the Dowager Countess and Mrs Hughes – have dropped their corsets. The fashionable figure is now boyish, straight up and down, and usually achieved with a girdle (a tight but flexible piece of underwear, reaching from just below the bosom to mid-thigh, like extra-extra-strength Spanx). For filming, the women may not wear period underwear unless it is seen on screen – 'Then you've got the opportunity to show as much detail as you like' – as the principal concern is ensuring that the actresses have the right lines, with no bumps or seams beneath their dresses.

For the fifth season, Anna was surprised to discover that most of the wardrobe would have to be designed from scratch. 'In series four, there was a lot of purple, the colour of half-mourning, and it affects the actors psychologically, it's too associated with death. So I've had to remove it, which meant I couldn't use much from the series, and anything from series three is really too old-fashioned. We did want as seamless a transition as possible, so some dresses have been reused, but far fewer than I thought we'd be able to.'

In many ways, moving from series four to five is like 'passing the baton in a relay race' says Anna. 'There can't be any jolts, but at the same time, we have to show that we're moving it forward.' Anna trawls vintage fairs at the weekends, carrying the actresses and their characters

in her mind. 'I'm plotting eighteen storylines at any one time, with a dozen dresses perhaps. Any costume has to be believable for the [aristocratic] family that they are and the wealth that they have – they would have had large wardrobes. Sometimes, if I'm out shopping, I'll spot things across the room – Edith and Rose speak to me very clearly. Edith is wearing fewer avant-garde outfits than she might have done because she's less in London, but I've still found her some amazing shoes. Mary is a dream to costume, but I want to make it all for her – I can never find anything ready-made that is beautiful enough, so her wardrobe is pretty much bespoke.'

Of course, just as they did back then, Anna tries to repeat outfits. 'You have to be clever where you repeat,' she explains. 'It happens now and again because we can't be like *Sex and the City*, where you never saw the same garment twice. On the other hand, the audiences want to see more and more ravishing costumes, so for our big set pieces, we dress everyone in new outfits.' The odd judicious piece of recycling happens too – a dressing gown that Carson is spotted wearing in an early episode of series five is an old one of Robert's.

Jewellery is provided by a single source – a hire house with huge stock: 'I can put an order in for what I need and either they've got it or it can be made. I'm also always finding things at the weekend vintage fairs. There's a lot more cut-steel and jet in the jewellery, and also hair accessories, as we move into 1924.'

Costume details from the set.

COSTUME CONTINUED

As well as being responsible for the many lavish and intricate dresses that the ladies wear, Anna is, of course, in charge of every other single stitch seen on screen, whether that's dressing a male cast member or someone in a crowd scene.

During series five, there is a scene in the village with fifty schoolchildren, which means having to do a lot of research just for that one short scene. Anna's resources include books – there's a particularly brilliant reference book, *1920s Fashion Design* by Pepin Press – but also the expertise sitting within the hire houses, such as Cosprop, with whom *Downton Abbey* has worked closely since the first series. Creating those crowd costumes often means making their own, so Anna has used a Savile Row-trained tailor and has a pool of other people she can call upon. 'It's a busy time for makers now, as there are a lot of film and television productions going on – if you're a good cutter and maker, you'll find yourself massively in demand. There are a lot working under full-time contracts too, which can create difficulties when I need things turned around within days.'

Every detail is checked for authenticity, as with this sergeant's stripes.

Alastair Bruce will sometimes advise a tweak to a costume. For example, a policeman will need a row of ribboned medals on his uniform – it's the kind of detail that research doesn't always throw up, but needs the specialist's eye. It's in touches like these that the show demonstrates its commitment to authenticity and telling small stories about how life was, almost subconsciously.

The men's wardrobes are smaller than the women's, but bring challenges of their own. 'We're trying to ring in the changes where we can,' says Anna. 'For example, Tony Gillingham is having a London suit made for this series – we've only really seen him in tweeds before, but now we're beginning to see him in a new light. Those suits bring with them a whole world of etiquette. We don't do so much for Robert, but at the same time, we can't leave him stuck in the past, we want to move him forward. So we'll just nudge it ahead a little bit, looking at the angle of the breast pocket, for example.'

Certain details might even cause Anna a restless night: 'I've got a specific obsession with ties. In a three-piece suit, there's a restriction on how much of a story we can tell with it, so the tie is what we can use to anchor that character. I'm always on the lookout for fabric that we can use to make ties. We use authentic 1920s ties where we can, but most of them are very worn out by now. And

what's funny is that men and women definitely choose different ties. If my wardrobe supervisor chooses a tie, you can bet that I'll prefer another!'

And while Anna has four washing machines constantly whirring away in her principal truck (there's also a 'crowd truck'), many of the men's clothes – particularly shirts and collars – have to be sent away to specialist cleaners, taking time that has to be scheduled in.

Below stairs, the changes in wardrobe move rather more slowly than above, being less influenced by fashion and more restricted by economies. Maids would traditionally have been given the cloth by the family – often as a Christmas present – in order to make their uniforms, whether themselves or by seamstresses. For the fifth series, all of the maids have had their day and evening dresses (not party dresses, but a uniform they would wear after their morning's work, when the dirtier chores of the day had been done) remade – the waists have been dropped and the hems raised a little. In the kitchen, the maids wear mobcaps and these have been shunted slightly forward – in the 1920s they would have worn them sitting almost on the forehead, but this was deemed to look a little too like pastiche and so, at Downton Abbey, they sit rather more at an angle instead. Mrs Patmore's uniform has changed slightly, an adjustment to the palette; Daisy's uniform is unique to her, as the only kitchen assistant. Despite the work they did, the maids would always be expected to look clean and presentable.

A lady's maid would sometimes be given old dresses by her mistress, and this is occasionally reflected in the show, but they are careful that this is done reasonably subtly, so that Anna, say, is not seen wearing something that is better suited to Mary's personality than hers. A lady's maid did not strictly wear uniforms, but had to dress simply, and certainly in a way that meant they couldn't be mistaken for their mistresses. Baxter has been given rather more complicated details in her dresses, because she is an extremely competent seamstress and would have enjoyed sewing those flourishes on to her own clothes. Mrs Hughes, for this series, has been given a new, rather stylish but still formidable, dark cashmere skirt and jacket, with a second suit made for the warmer summer episodes.

Carson's uniform has not changed one iota since the first series – nor would it have for any butler working from the late Victorian years into the 1920s: a morning coat for the day, white tie for evening. The footmen would be decked out in livery, often made at Savile Row – they were deemed to be the showpieces for the house and it was important that they looked smart, with details such as the family's crest on their buttons. Many houses would keep several footmen's liveries, in case they brought in extra men to serve at larger dinners or to line a staircase at a London party – if you find forty liveries in a stately home's cupboard, it doesn't, therefore, mean that they once had forty footmen working there. As with the lady's maids, valets often wore cast-offs from their master; indeed, for many, it was a perk of the job.

With Anna's designs for the show authentic and yet appealing to the modern eye, it's not surprising the actors covet their own costumes in a twenty-first-century twist on the perk. As Anna says, 'Our bespoke shoes are turning heads. Lady Rose's blue Mary Janes with twisted pipe straps and Edith's heeled brogues are so on-trend. And there are always some beautiful original beaded gowns that look so stunning, the girls can see themselves on the red carpet in them…' We'll be watching.

Tim Drewe as chief estate fireman.

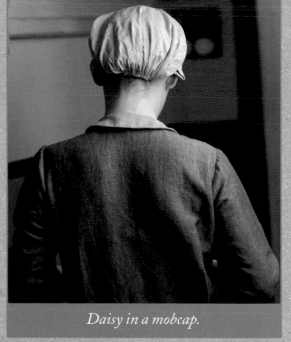

Daisy in a mobcap.

JULY

Summer

THE EARL
OF GRANTHAM
(Robert)

JULY

The thwack of a cricket ball on a willow bat, the taste of strawberries and cream, the smell of freshly cut grass and the first sight of the sea: these are all happy reminders of an English summer.

This is not to say that an actual 'summer' is always guaranteed, but it is always welcome, particularly by those at Downton Abbey. When you live, as they do, in Yorkshire – a county not noted for its warm weather at any time of year – you learn to get your thrills without relying on the sunshine.

The Crawleys and families like them did not take trips in the way that we do today. Visits to relations across Europe would happen at any time of the year and the summer was often something to be enjoyed at home. Places that we think of now as fashionable summer resorts, such as the Riviera or Capri, were actually winter destinations; it was not until 1931 that the hotels in Cannes, for example, were persuaded to stay open in the summer months. Instead, the month of July meant pleasure on one's own estate, playing gentle sports – croquet, tennis, cricket... There might be picnics, although Violet finds it rather extraordinary that a lady of her position is expected to attend such events – in the eighteenth and nineteenth centuries these were the sort of occasions that were considered the pastime of a shepherd or farm labourer – but they had begun to be fashionable in the 1920s. If members of the upper class did have picnics, they were still prepared by the cook and served by a footman. An aristocratic unmarried man and woman would not have a jolly picnic together in the park.

All the year round, the servants lived a simple life of mainly work and little play. Reflecting this, their one private space, their bedroom, may have had one or two personal touches, but would otherwise have been as it was found when they first arrived – a bed, a wardrobe, a chest of drawers, perhaps a marble washstand with a jug and basin. There might have been one or two pictures hanging on the walls, usually of a religious or nature scene. In the 1920s, perhaps one or two of the younger maids would have pulled out pictures from the new Hollywood magazines.

THE RECOMMENDED MENU FOR A PICNIC

FROM ETIQUETTE OF GOOD SOCIETY BY LADY COLIN CAMPBELL, 1893

FOR AN OUTDOOR LUNCHEON

The following list of provisions will be found the most suitable: Cold roast beef, ribs and shoulder of lamb, roast fowls, ducks, ham, pressed tongue; beefsteak, pigeon and grouse pies, game, veal patties, lobsters, cucumbers and lettuces for salad, cheese-cakes, jam or marmalade turnovers, stewed fruit in bottles, bottle of cream, college puddings, blancmange in mould, plain biscuits to eat with fruit and cheese, rolls, butter, cream cheese, and fresh fruit. Bottled beer and porter, claret, sherry, champagne, soda-water, lemonade, cherry-brandy.

FOR TEA

Loaves of bread, sponge-cakes, plum-cakes, buns, rolls, butter, potted fish and meats, tongue, cheese-cakes, plain and sweet biscuits, fruit, bottle of cream, and tea. It is useless to attempt to make coffee on an occasion of this kind, unless the company is capable of appreciating the fragrant berry in its best form, i.e. Turkish coffee, which can be made to perfection in an ordinary saucepan, where it should be allowed just to come to boiling point three times in succession, and then served while the rich brown foam is still on the surface.

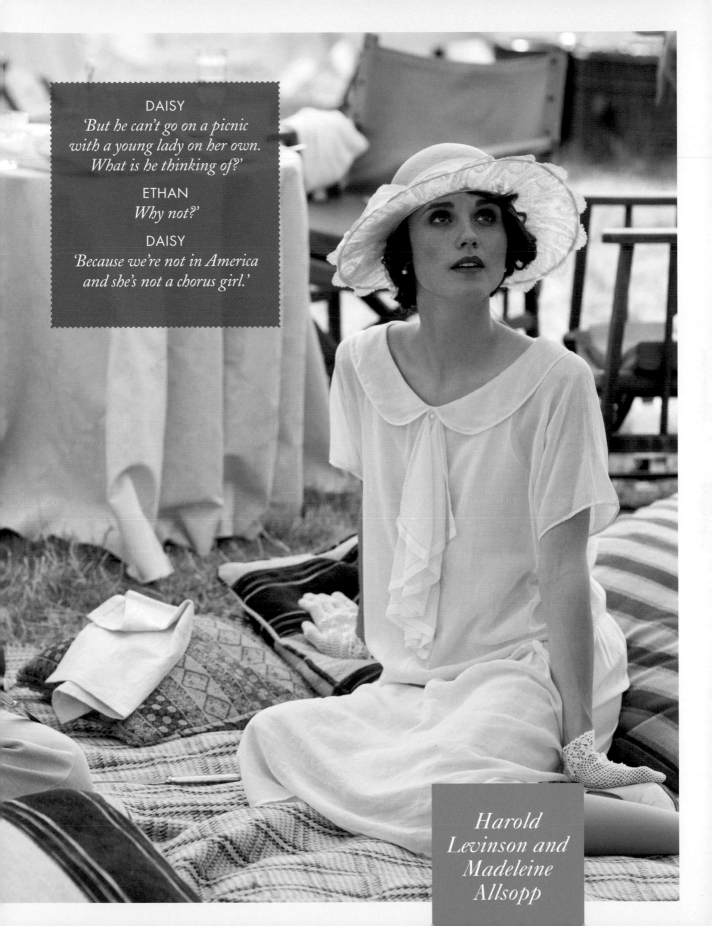

DAISY
'But he can't go on a picnic
with a young lady on her own.
What is he thinking of?'

ETHAN
'Why not?'

DAISY
'Because we're not in America
and she's not a chorus girl.'

Harold
Levinson and
Madeleine
Allsopp

These remote, bare rooms at the top of vast houses were a world away from the small, busy cottages that most of the servants would have grown up in. They tended to come from farming families, where there were normally several siblings and a mother who was always cooking in the kitchen and trying to keep her children in order. Coming from such homes, with their low ceilings and cramped furniture, and the family squeezed into just two or three rooms, a young person entering service and moving to a house like Downton Abbey would often have felt quite a culture shock. But they would, at least, have been used to the long hours and hard work expected of them. Servants generally got an afternoon off a week and a week's holiday each year. Their day was not relentless from dawn to dusk – there were proper breaks for each meal – but there was little room for private occupations or interests. At least in the summer, Carson is more inclined – even if only slightly more – to give the staff a break when the fair comes to town.

For special occasions, the servants travel to Ripon to kit themselves out with a new item or two – Mrs Patmore treats herself to a new shirt from Mrs Curley's dress shop when the grocer asks her to Thirsk fair. The fairs are a joy to watch in the show, with their merry-go-rounds and tug-of-war competitions. Fairs would have been set up by travelling companies, much as they are now, arriving at the same time each year.

'No, I won't be coming. If I came, they wouldn't have fun. They'd spend the day looking over their shoulder.'

CARSON

Mrs Patmore and the villagers enjoy a day out at the fair.

LEMON BARLEY WATER

This was always on offer for the women after dinner and it also makes a wonderfully refreshing beverage for the summer months.

SERVES 4–6

100g pearl barley
juice of 2 lemons
caster sugar, to taste
(about 6 teaspoons)

Place the barley in a sieve and rinse under cold water until the water runs clear.

Put the barley into a saucepan with 1.2 litres of fresh water and bring to the boil. Simmer slowly for 20 minutes.

Strain the liquid into a jug (save the barley to use in a salad or soup) and add the lemon juice. Add sugar to taste and leave to cool to room temperature. Then transfer to the fridge to chill until needed.

*Anna and Baxter
in a light-hearted moment.*

Summer for the servants would have meant long hours in the fields when they were growing up; their work in the house may have been easier on the back, but there would have been a pang from one or two of them for the nostalgic pleasure of chewing a stalk of grass as they lay on the top of a hay bale as the sun set. These warmer months, too, heralded a holiday for some – a few days' leave to allow them to get back home to see their families.

But even for the servants not going home, the summer months brought a break to their routine, as the estate got involved in traditional events, from flower shows to church bazaars and garden fêtes. There may even have been an outing or two in the offing, whether to the travelling fair when it came to the village or even the seaside.

Mixed reactions to the sack race from Cora and Carson.

Local village events, such as flower shows, cricket matches and church bazaars, would often fall under the jurisdiction of the big house – partly because to have the local nobility hand out the prizes was seen as lending glamour and credence to any occasion and partly because they were able to host some of the events on their estate. The garden at Downton Abbey is considerably larger than the village green.

Hosting an event also means that Cora and Robert are unofficially elected to preside over the squabbling factions every village had. Despite her complaints, when called to organise a garden fête or church bazaar, Cora appears to enjoy the task in hand – they are a reminder of the war years, which she would never say publicly were happy years, but they were certainly a time when she had purpose, feeling both useful and busy.

'What a nightmare. The man selling ices is ill, so I've got to find another. And the grocers from Easingwold and Malton can't be side by side, and now I've got to decide the house menus with Mrs Patmore.'

CORA

Molesley serves Master George and Miss Sybbie strawberries and cream.

The whole village pulls behind the bazaar, with cakes made by the local women for the cake stall, a flower stand of locally grown flowers and a Downton Abbey table with produce from the home farm. The footmen are roped in to serve punch and tea; Mrs Patmore makes sandwiches and provides beer for the estate workers setting up the tables. Even Lady Mary pulls her weight.

PIMM'S CUP

What could be more welcome on a warm English summer's day than a cold glass of Pimm's? Invented in 1840, it is still the refreshment of choice at garden parties, and while watching a cricket Test match or the tennis at Wimbledon.

MAKES 1 LARGE JUG

a handful of strawberries
½ orange
¼ cucumber
a bunch of mint leaves
250ml Pimm's No. 1
500ml lemonade
250ml ginger ale
plenty of ice

Hull and slice the strawberries and cut the orange into thin slices. Cut the cucumber in half lengthways and then into thin slices. Chop the mint.

Pour the Pimm's into a large jug or bowl, followed by the lemonade and ginger ale. Add the strawberries, orange, cucumber and mint to the jug. Top up with ice and stir with a long spoon.

Pour into glasses to serve.

SCONES

These little scones are best eaten while still slightly warm, split and spread with lashings
of clotted or whipped cream and homemade strawberry jam.
A large pot of tea is the requisite accompaniment.

**MAKES ABOUT
18 SMALL SCONES**

450g self-raising flour,
plus extra for dusting
2 teaspoons baking powder
a pinch of salt
100g butter, at room
temperature
4 tablespoons caster sugar
250ml milk

Preheat the oven to 230°C/450°F/gas 8. Lightly dust a large baking sheet with flour.

Sieve the flour, baking powder and salt into a large bowl and stir well. Crumble in the butter and rub it into the flour with your fingertips to make fine crumbs. Stir in the sugar. Using a fork, stir in the milk gradually – just enough to bring it into a soft, slightly sticky dough, which you should handle as little as possible. Add a drop more milk or a little more flour if necessary.

Sprinkle some flour over your worktop and turn the dough out on to it. Flour your hands and bring the dough into a ball. Using a lightly floured rolling pin, roll the dough out to a thickness of 2cm. Using a 5cm cutter, stamp out a round and place it on the baking sheet. Cut out as many more scones as you can. Bring the remaining scraps of dough into a ball and roll out again to make the last few scones.

Dust the scones with flour and bake in the centre of the oven for 10 minutes or until well risen and golden. Cool on a wire rack.

CARSON: *'So. We decorate the stalls today – you all know the drill. And remember anything shabby shows Downton in a bad light.'*

MRS HUGHES: *'And we can't have that.'*

CARSON: *'No, Mrs Hughes. We can't.'*

Events such as these were designed to bring together the house, its servants and estate workers, as well as the villagers. In many ways, it was a reminder of the feudal system, when the local big house and its lord and lady were the king and queen of the miniature realm. By 1924, that social structure was, thankfully, no longer in place, but there's still no question that such events were a highlight of the year in a time before television and budget airlines provided entertainment and holidays.

Carson, of course, is still minded to treat the event as a feudal one, keen that the great house must be seen as being as grand and well run as any royal palace.

Then again, Carson finds the notion that a servant might have any kind of life or interest beyond Downton hard to understand. Fortunately, Mrs Hughes is rather more sympathetic to the younger ones and will nudge him to allow the others to enjoy some time away now and then. By the mid-1920s, the servants are able to catch a late-night screening at the local cinema (there were showings especially for servants, at 10 p.m., when their duties would be over). Jimmy goes to see *The Sheik*, starring the Hollywood idol of the day, Rudolph Valentino.

Badminton
at Downton
Abbey.

ANNA: *'Is there anything I could do to make up for it?'*

BATES: *'Hmm. Let me think… You could always buy me a penny lick.'*

In summer 1923, after a few hard weeks in London for the season, the Downton servants are given the chance to indulge in a special outing. Rejecting Carson's initial idea to visit the museums of London, they take the train to the seaside – the beautiful Pullman from Victoria would have taken them straight to Brighton. All the traditional seaside fun would be had, with ice-cream stalls selling penny licks, mechanical dolls that moved when you put in sixpence, Pierrots miming and fortune-tellers waving their hands over crystal balls.

Lavinia Smiley recollected one terrifying daily event: 'A stout lady who twice a day dived off the highest place at the very end of the pier. Her most spectacular turn was to get into a sack that had been dipped in petrol with just her head sticking out. Somebody set a match to her, and wreathed in flames she jumped – about sixty feet – into the sea below.'

Sitting on the beach or on one of the deckchairs that could be hired for the day, dipping into a wicker basket with sandwiches and drinking from a flask of lemonade, some might even brave the sea itself. Bathing costumes – as swimsuits were called then – would be put on just before going into the water; they were designed to preserve a lady or gentleman's modesty and certainly did not allow them to cut a very aquiline figure. Children often wore rubber garments called 'paddlers' to stop them getting too wet, though the sand would invariably get in and cause a nasty itch. For those who didn't want to get completely wet and bother with the awkward business of changing behind a windbreak or in a tiny seaside hut, they could always just take their shoes off, roll up their trousers and go for a paddle. As we rather touchingly saw Carson and Mrs Hughes do in the final scene of series four: the stately pair wade out carefully into the briny froth, watched, with great amusement, by the others.

Life's a beach for Thomas.

A day at the seaside.

MRS HUGHES: *'You can hold my hand. Then we'll both go in together.'*

CARSON: *'I think I will hold your hand. It'll make me feel a bit steadier.'*

MRS HUGHES: *'You can always hold my hand if you need to feel steady.'*

CARSON: *'I don't know how, but you manage to make that sound a little risqué.'*

MRS HUGHES: *'And if I did? We're getting on, Mr Carson, you and I. We can afford to live a little.'*

PROPS

There are several elements that make *Downton Abbey* a highly watchable television series, from its compelling plots to the award-winning acting. But one of the key factors is that the audience trusts that it is watching an authentic account of life in that period. The Crawleys and their servants may have more than their fair share of troubles, but they suffer them in a house that is unquestionably one of an aristocratic family's in the early twentieth century. A large part of this is down to the fact that the location in which the above-stairs scenes are filmed is the house of an aristocratic family, one that has lived there for over 300 years. Nevertheless, the house as it is seen on screen is not exactly as it looks in real life and, of course, every other location is either an entirely constructed set – as with the whole of the servants' quarters, built at Ealing Studios – or another house, adapted for *Downton* purposes. It is essential that everything seamlessly joins together and appears to be exactly right for 1924, so that the viewers are able to trust in what is happening on screen and allow themselves to sink happily into the drama.

A vintage fan from series five.

Linda Wilson is the set decorator, selecting all the props from beds to matchboxes, lights to drapes and so on, after Donal Woods and the director have briefed her. Linda is one part of a large art department that works apparently seamlessly to bring the visual elements of the show to the screen. Supervising art director Mark Kebby is responsible for overall logistics and planning, as well as being the show's lead draughtsman. Art director Chantelle Valentine is mainly responsible for graphics and co-ordinating vehicles with Michael Geary, who provides all the cars. There is also a standby art director on set at all times, an art department assistant/runner, production buyer, assistant buyer, construction manager, property master, dressing propmen, standby propmen, painters, carpenters and prop makers.

New to the show for series five, Linda was already a fan and started to prep just before Christmas 2013, reading the scripts and looking through the continuity pictures: 'A lot of things have been purchased for the show over the years, or certain things hired are set in stone, so I have to get those things back in again and re-dress them to the standards that have been set.'

Linda uses either her own large reference library – 'I've got hundreds of books at home' – or turns to the internet to check whether or not a prop will be right. 'You start to get a feel for the year, but you also learn about how those houses operated and bring that to the set,' she says. 'Such as thinking about where the vegetables for the kitchen will have been sourced and where the flowers will have been picked.' There are less obvious starting points too: 'Sometimes you look at paintings to get an idea for colours, or go to a National Trust building to see how objects are arranged or pictures are hung,' she says. 'What's amazing about *Downton* is that you're entering a body of work – because it's been going for a few years now, it's a reference of its own.'

While things that are used from year to year have been bought and are owned by the production – such as the Household Wants Indicator in the kitchen or some of the personal items in the bedrooms – a great many come from prop houses, quite a few of which are handily close to Ealing Studios, in Acton, west London. These companies constantly add to their collections and will find items that are authentically of the period. They are particularly helpful when Linda has to build an entirely new set, such as a chemist's shop ('I hired bottles from five different places') or cake shop.

Linda is a keen gardener outside of her work and enjoys dressing the house with flowers. 'Whenever we do a dining-room or drinks-party scene, it's lovely to use fresh flowers and make a great show of it. We think Cora would be appreciative of the effort.' But everything has to be thought through or a mistake could easily find its way on to the screen: 'In the wartime, for example, people grew more vegetables rather than flowers for the house.'

The kitchen is often the starting point for small stories told by the props. 'Directors usually have a clear idea as to what they'd like the actors to be doing and I'll stand by on set and see how the lemons should be cut or eggs broken,' says Linda. 'But we try to come up with ideas too, so it's more interesting. For instance, there was a scene where the kitchen maids were making chocolates and then later, in the dining room, we saw the family eating them. Whether or not the viewer picks up on these details, it helps everything appear real.'

On a shooting day, Linda will always be working ahead, preparing sets one or two days before filming. 'We've been dressing the Dower House today, which has been recreated on set at Ealing. We've been steam-cleaning the curtains and putting the hawthorn bushes out in the garden. I'm also researching for episodes six and seven, beginning to make phone calls and put out enquiries for things we'll need. We've got a team of three to make sure all props and continuity props are in on time.'

Next time you watch a scene in the show, consider the fact that every item in the background has been deliberately thought about and put in its place. 'Nothing is there accidentally,' says Linda. 'Even at Highclere, we don't just walk in and it's all in place. We take out their furniture and put in our furniture. It's wonderful to link the different places together – starting in the castle and going down to the kitchens. We're always very busy and we get going early in the morning.' And with that, Linda presses on with her fascinating and eventful working day.

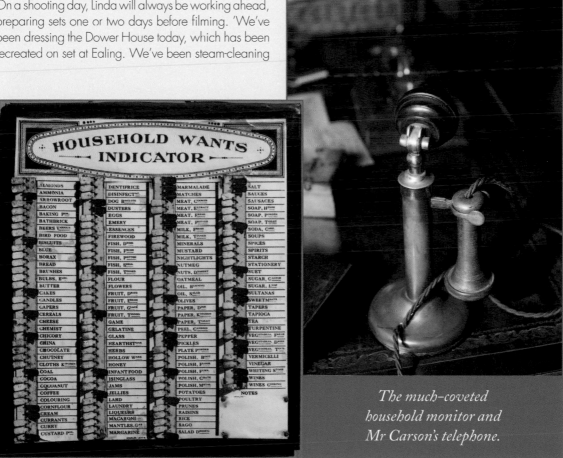

The much-coveted household monitor and Mr Carson's telephone.

AUGUST
Scotland

AUGUST

As the world changes around her at a rate she can neither understand nor keep up with, there is always one haven for the likes of Violet, our Dowager Countess: Scotland. Whether it is the ancient traditions, the centuries-old heather growing on the sleeping hills or the reassuringly cold comforts of a Scottish castle, a retreat among tartan-clad relations is to be relished; a charming reminder of times past. Examining the Crawleys' departure to their cousins, the Marquess and Marchioness of Flintshire (Susan is Violet's niece), is a welcome opportunity for us to look at the old ways, something which Violet, above all, enjoys.

The journey to Duneagle Castle begins at Downton Station, where the family and their servants board the train. Anna and Bates, as lady's maid and valet, are happily able to enjoy the trip as a small holiday of their own (for O'Brien, however, Cora's lady's maid at the time, this is work as usual); Bates admits to a Scottish ancestry – his mother was a Keith.

Much to Robert's consternation, his dog Isis must be left behind, in the care of Tom Branson, who hasn't been invited, which worries Violet: 'I know he's housebroken more or less, but I don't want freedom to go to his head.' Turns out, as with so many things, she is right.

Lavinia Smiley remembered her own family's Scottish expeditions when she was a child, in the 1920s, travelling up from King's Cross Station and occupying almost an entire carriage of first-class sleepers. The children would struggle to wake up in time to look out of the window as they crossed the magnificent Forth Bridge: 'It was like going into a new world. For many years all the taxis waiting at Aberdeen Station were Rolls-Royces – demoted from a more gracious castle life among the lairds, I suppose – and in one (or two) of them we would be driven the fifteen miles through rolling farmland to Dunecht.' Lavinia recalled that her aunt's maid had to arrive at the station well before her ladyship, in order to make up the bed in the sleeping car with linen sheets. Thankfully, even Violet is rather less demanding.

Mrs. Hamilton Stephenson
née Isie Madeléne Fellowes
1880—1971

This is a portrait of Julian's great-aunt, Isie Stephenson (1880-1971). She was the original inspiration behind Violet, even providing some of her best lines, such as 'What is a weekend?'

Violet's character was inspired by Julian's paternal great-aunt, Isie. Born in 1880 (rather later than Violet, who was a child of the 1850s), she married the heir to a rubber fortune, Hamilton Stephenson, always known as Bertie. Bertie descended from a cherished illegitimate son of a Regency Duke of Norfolk who hated his wife (whom he divorced in 1794) and loved his mistress. He enriched the child, marrying him off to Lady Mary Keppel, daughter of the 4th Earl of Albemarle. Bertie's first cousin was Harold Nicolson, husband to Vita Sackville-West, famed in the 1920s for her intimate female friendships, most particularly with Virginia Woolf. 'All in all, by her own admission, she [Isie] had married into a pretty tangled and very interesting group,' says Julian.

'We country dwellers must beware of being too provincial.'
VIOLET

Isie was named after her much-loved aunt, Eliza, always known as Isie, who died of consumption within a month of her niece's birth. 'She really functioned as our paternal grandmother, as our real one was pretty mad and detested children,' says Julian, who today owns a portrait of her as a child, as well as this pretty watercolour of her grown up and a miniature painted for her fiancé to keep on their engagement.

Tragically, Isie's husband died of wounds in the First World War, and her only son, Russell, drowned in the Second. It was Isie who originally said to Julian a line he later gave to Sybil in the second series; she had gone to a ball after the war and on entering the room, thought she must have mistakenly come to a hen party, as she could see only women. Gradually, she spotted a man here and there and realised that men had been invited – it was simply that there were almost no men left. 'It was as if every man you ever danced with was dead,' she said.

Violet shares with Isie her formidable air, a belief in the aristocracy's right to reign and a certain severe snobbishness, but as Julian has said, the women of that time were complex. They had been brought up to believe that life held sure things for them, as it had for their mothers, grandmothers and great-grandmothers. As young women, their expectations were solid, but the world they grew up in was shattered by the war. Their education and upbringing had apparently failed to prepare them for this. In fact, women of Isie and Violet's generation were prepared for little more than marriage, for that was what was to bring them independence from their parents, operating their social and charitable lives from their husband's grand houses. Isie told a wonderful story of her own education, in which she was walked around the garden by her governess. They would pause by every shrub and Isie would have to spontaneously introduce a new topic of conversation. The idea was that you would be able to keep a party going even if the people you were with had all the social abilities of a plant.

Nevertheless, women of Isie and Violet's type could be tough – they were the undisputed matriarchs and ruled their houses. They bring to mind a line from a memoir in which a young nanny recalls the aristocratic grandmother, Lady Reeve: '[She] had a direct manner of speaking. She acknowledged two superiors – God and Queen Victoria.' These women had one certain priority: family. For Violet, even when her granddaughter Mary has behaved in ways which must be shocking to someone of her own generation, she will stand by her, no matter what, because she is family. Violet and Al Capone share one or two qualities, it may be said.

Violet is, of course, played by Dame Maggie Smith, an actress who commands great respect, not just from her immediate *Downton Abbey* family, but from audiences worldwide. She came to international attention for the eponymous, Oscar-winning role in *The Prime of Miss Jean Brodie,* directed, coincidentally, by Gareth's late grandfather Ronald. Maggie Smith is shrug-the-shoulder modest about her career: 'One went to school, one wanted to act, one started to act and one's still acting.'

Gareth has said of Maggie: 'It probably goes without saying she's a huge part of Downton and has received accolade after accolade for it. And I think she enjoys doing the show. It's remarkable that someone who's had such a long and illustrious career continues to deliver work of this calibre. And in reflecting on the pivotal role that she plays, one ought to mention the extraordinary collaboration of Maggie Smith and Julian Fellowes. She's almost like a muse to him.' As Maggie has said, Violet is, in fact, 'the third old lady I've played for him, so I am getting the hang of it now'. (She was Lady Trentham in *Gosford Park* and Mrs Oldknow in *From Time to Time.*) The two of them certainly enjoy quick-witted banter and Julian has said that he enjoys writing for her because her timing is immaculate; nothing has to be explained about the beat or intention of a line: 'I write a line that I think is quite funny, then she says it and it's hilarious.'

On set, Maggie is adored by her fellow cast, and she certainly doesn't have the same prickly relationship with Penelope Wilton as Violet does with Isobel Crawley – they are often seen taking strolls together around the grounds of Highclere. Her younger fellow actors will confess to feelings of apprehension before first filming a scene with Maggie, which she soon dispels with a remark of either reassurance or wit. It might be a surprise to some – if not all! – to hear that Maggie herself has confessed to feelings of nerves. One reporter once asked her if, when she was sitting there as Violet, in an incredible hat, she was nervous. 'Like a lump of jelly,' she replied. 'Worried that if I don't get this speech right, I'm done for.'

Maggie Smith and Penelope Wilton on location.

While the end of the London Season was traditionally marked by the beginning of the Scottish sporting season on the Glorious Twelfth (the name for the start of the grouse season), on our screens, we see the Crawleys go to the Highlands for stalking early in September, as the first signs of autumn begin to show. The episode – the finale for series three – was filmed in late July and early August and the costume designer then, Caroline McCall, had prepared herself for grim weather (it's always raining in Scotland), 'but it was really beautiful', she laughs.

Caroline dressed the principal actors in earthy green colours, with Mary in burgundy. 'I wanted to have a change [from the family at home in Downton] and to show the passage of time. We'd last seen them at the summer cricket match and now it was autumnal, with Mary pregnant,' she explains. Of course, a little tartan wouldn't go amiss and would be entirely in keeping. Many families liked to reference their ancestry if they were able. One child remembered being dressed in green and black Dunecht tweed for her holiday, her grandmother rumoured to have bought a mile of it: 'There was something rather pleasant about being dressed the same as all the retainers – keepers, ghillies, gardeners and even the dour old groom.'

Much of the kit, however, was sporting in nature – and not just for the men. Increasingly, in the 1920s, ladies were joining in, particularly with fishing. Women were always reputed to be the best salmon-catchers on the Scotch rivers and Lady Colin Campbell, in her book *Etiquette of Good Society*, was very precise about what the smart lady-angler should wear: 'A kilt skirt of rough tweed unheeded and reaching a little below the knee, over a pair of tweed knickerbockers to match, a Norfolk jacket with plenty of pockets, ribbed woollen stockings, stout low-heeled shoes and a deerstalker cap, form the best and most workmanlike costume for a woman to go fishing in.'

However, the author clearly did not believe women were able to handle all the aspects of fly-fishing: 'A man should be taken for the purpose of baiting the hooks and taking off the fish when caught.'

The filming of the episode took place in Inveraray (pronounced 'Inverara') Castle in the West Highlands, owned by friends of Alastair Bruce, the Duke and Duchess of Argyll: 'They're lovely people and they had said to me that if *Downton* should ever go to Scotland, they'd love to provide the location. It's a romantic place, so when Julian said he was thinking of doing a Scottish episode for the season finale, I passed the message along!' Alastair also became rather closely involved with the stalking scenes: 'Where [the actors and director] needed specific advice was on the hills. So I was on the spot as the ghillie [a Scottish gamekeeper].' Resplendent with a long beard, too. Alastair was also quite literally on hand for the fishing: 'I was there at the riverside, where I repeatedly picked up a dead fish [in the background] until the gill snapped – I had to stop the filming, I was laughing so much.'

'They've earned our respect and they deserve a clean death.'

NIELD (GAMEKEEPER)

Before the sport begins, the family is awoken by the strains of a bagpipe drifting in at the windows – melodious or not, depending on your particular point of view. With several guests staying in the house party and a long day of stalking ahead, a magnificent breakfast would always be laid on. One guest remembered, years later, a repast that still seemed to make her mouth water: 'porridge with the thickest cream and eggs and bacon and sausages, and herrings in oatmeal, and heather honey spread on baps'.

After a hearty breakfast, the men would travel on the wagonette (an open horse car with springs) to the first hill. Accompanied by the ghillie, they'd spend several hours crawling through the heather in search of a stag. The sport was largely born out of a need to cull the deer population, which would otherwise damage crops and gardens. There is strict emphasis on the need for a clean kill – the aim is always to kill the animal with a single shot, so accuracy is paramount. If you are unable to aim precisely, thanks to an obstruction or because the deer is moving too fast, then you may not fire your rifle. This can, of course, lead to many hours of no action at all.

As well as stalking, the men would go fly-fishing too. To partake in field sports was seen as the mark of a gentleman and although most sport enjoyed by the upper classes seemed to involve hunting and killing mammals, birds and fish, a new, rather more harmless leisure pursuit was beginning to gain ground amongst the upper classes: golf (which they pronounced 'goff').

Train travel, in the late Victorian age, meant people could travel to Scotland – birthplace of golf – more easily than ever before and so the pastime spread. Gleneagles Hotel, now famed worldwide for being one of the best examples of a golf hotel and course, opened in June 1924.

After a morning at the castle, the women would perhaps have a ladies' luncheon by the loch, riding in a rather bumpy trap through the glen to get there. As Mary says: 'We were shaken around in that trap like dice in a cup.' Usually the men wouldn't join them, but if they were having a particularly miserable sporting day, then they could, of course.

Anna and Bates, beholden though they are to the needs of their master and mistress, are able to sneak off for a picnic by a river. It's a rare delight and should be savoured. Except for the fact that one of the real difficulties with picnicking in Scotland is the presence of midges – swarms of tiny, biting insects that come out with the sunshine. But there are moments in the day when the midges aren't too terrible, the rainclouds have drifted elsewhere and the sun warms one's face. Anna packs a couple of beers, simple sandwiches, cheese and fruit, cadged from the cook. They only want a little sustenance to be enjoyed al fresco, away from the formalities of the servants' hall table. The servants know well how to cherish such small moments of pleasure at Downton Abbey throughout the year.

SCOTTISH SHORTBREAD

Shortbread is said to have originated in Scotland and may well have formed part of Anna and Bates's picnic. It is delicious with creamy English puddings such as fruit fools or simply with a cup of tea.

MAKES 8 WEDGES

125g plain flour
30g fine semolina
   or ground rice
a pinch of salt
50g caster sugar, plus extra
   for sprinkling
100g cold unsalted butter

Preheat the oven to 160°C/325°F/gas 3. You will need a 20cm round, shallow cake tin.

Sieve the flour, semolina and salt into a mixing bowl. Stir in the caster sugar. Crumble the butter into the bowl and rub into the dry mixture with your fingertips to make fine crumbs.

Knead the mixture together with your hands until you have a smooth, dough-like texture. Place in the middle of the cake tin. Using your hands, press the mixture out to fill the tin in an even layer.

Bake in the oven for 15–20 minutes, until the shortbread is slightly coloured. Remove from the oven and leave to stand in the tin for 10 minutes until the shortbread has firmed up a little but is still warm. Cut into wedges, sprinkle with caster sugar and leave to cool and harden in the tin.

SPICED BEEF

*Also known as huntsman's beef, this is sliced thinly and eaten cold –
just the thing for picnics, sandwiches and shooting lunches.*

SERVES 10–12

1.5–2kg piece of rolled
  and boned beef brisket
  or topside
1 tablespoon black
  peppercorns
1 tablespoon whole allspice
1 tablespoon juniper berries
10g saltpetre
100g sea salt
80g dark brown muscovado
  sugar

Place the beef in an ovenproof, lidded dish that fits it as snugly
as possible.

Grind the peppercorns, allspice and juniper berries in a spice
grinder. Mix with the saltpetre, sea salt and sugar. Rub this mixture
all over the beef. Cover and leave in the fridge for 7–10 days,
turning once a day.

When this time has passed, preheat the oven to 140°C/275°F/gas 1.
Remove the beef from the dish and wipe off the spices and juices.
Rinse out the dish and place the beef back in it. Cover tightly
with two layers of foil, place the lid on top and cook in the oven
for 3 hours.

Remove the beef from the oven and leave to cool for 3 hours in its
dish. Then drain the fat and wipe the beef with kitchen paper. Wrap
it in clingfilm and place on a board. Put another board on top of
the beef and place heavy weights on top. Refrigerate for 24 hours.
Remove the board and weights, rewrap the beef in clingfilm or foil
and refrigerate until needed. It will keep for up to 2 weeks.

For the Downton young, the highlight of the Scottish trip is the Ghillies Ball. Attended by the family and their senior servants, it's a lively night. Violet remembers going to her first Ghillies Ball, at Balmoral, in 1860: 'All the men were as tight as ticks!' Today, the Queen and the Duke of Edinburgh still hold a Ghillies Ball during their summer stay at Balmoral, inviting the castle staff and the local community and traditionally kick off proceedings by dancing an eightsome reel with three other couples.

The dances are not always easy to learn, but are huge fun. The names of the reels alone are enticing: Dashing White Sergeant, Gay Gordons, Robertson Rant, Hooper's Jig, to name but a very few. Lady Rose, who would have been reeling as soon as she could walk, teaches Anna one or two of the dances, so that she may impress her husband, Bates. And so she duly does.

ALASTAIR BRUCE

HISTORICAL ADVISOR

At Downton Abbey, no man is seen with his hands in his pockets, the women sit at the dining table with their hands on their laps and you'll never hear 'either' or 'neither' pronounced as 'ee-ther' or 'nee-ther' (which began only after the American soldiers came to Britain during the Second World War). These small but essential details – and hundreds of others – are down to one man: Alastair Bruce, *Downton Abbey*'s historical advisor.

Alastair is usually to be found on set, watching the monitors as each scene is shot. Afterwards, he'll leap up to have a word in the first assistant director's ear: 'Could you perhaps give a note to Sophie [McShera] that the dish she is holding is worth thousands of pounds, so perhaps better not to dump it down?' But he's crucial at most of the production stages, particularly in the line-up. This is when it is decided how the scene is going to go, with the director, actors, director of photography (for the lighting), the producer (Chris Croucher) and Alastair. At this point, the actors run through the lines and block exactly where they will move. Then there is a crew show (for the cameramen, costume, hair and make-up), so they can all see what the action's going to be and what the extras will do. Alastair helps the first AD with this detail in particular.

Alastair Bruce doubles up as the Lord Chamberlain and historical advisor.

O n set at Ealing Studios, Alastair watches a breakfast scene being filmed in the servants' hall. The centre of the action is Carson, as he hands out the post to the rest of the servants, and he has a short conversation with Molesley. But Alastair has his eye on the non-speaking parts, checking the tiny details the audience may hardly realise they are taking in, but which all add up to the bigger picture of portraying what life was really like in a house like Downton Abbey. Of the scene being filmed, Alastair explains: 'I'm very proud of the bell ringing at the start, because I don't think we hear them enough. They would be too distracting [for the television viewer], but the fact is that in a house like this, the bells would be ringing all the time. See here in the background – a kitchen maid comes out and signals with a small nod of her head that Carson's breakfast is ready and then we see the hall boy deliver his scrambled eggs [after the food stylist has checked with Alastair that they could sprinkle a little fresh parsley on first]. This story underlines that hall boys were in training to be footmen. So there are always hidden narratives going on.'

Alastair's expertise means he notices things that others might not. He points to the monitor, where the camera is showing a hall boy holding a cup of tea: 'We've had this problem before. The actor is left-handed, but it simply wouldn't have been allowed in 1924.'

Alastair Bruce of Crionaich, to give him his full, somewhat unpronounceable name, is a direct descendant of Robert the Bruce and has several areas of expertise. As the royal, religious and national events commentator for Sky News, he had to drop *Downton* for a few days when Lady Thatcher died, in order to cover her funeral. He holds the title of Colonel of the Reservists in London (having seen active service in the Falklands War), as well as Fitzalan Pursuivant of Arms Extraordinary, which means he leads the royal procession for the State Opening of Parliament; and he works with the Garter King of Arms on royal heraldry, designing the Middleton coat of arms (as well as the Crawley crest for the show). Since HRH Prince Edward was twenty-four years old, Alastair has been his equerry and he is ambassador for the Hampshire Scouts. He's even recently been awarded a professorship by Winchester University, of which he is as proud as his OBE.

Alastair's knowledge of the minutiae of the *Downton* world comes from his study of court life from the end of the 1700s to 1945: 'Aristocracy apes that, to greater or lesser effect, depending on the money available.' He sees his job as giving suggestions to the directors, but they can do with those what they will: 'I'm treading a fine line between authenticity and practical reality – it's entertainment, not historical documentary. But we show we know what we're doing in the details and give psychological confidence to the viewer in what they're watching.'

Alastair comes to the scripts quite late in the process, although Julian will sometimes discuss ideas at an earlier stage. 'I sit between the titans [Gareth Neame, Julian Fellowes and Liz Trubridge] and help them reach the point they want to get to,' he says. Scripts in hand, Alastair will sit with the first AD to work out what supporting actors will be needed, 'so that a door can be properly opened or a car arrives or luggage is taken, meaning that any scene set in any room is delivered in the form in which it would have happened'.

But perhaps the most fun Alastair has had on set has been as an extra, appearing, in almost Hitchcockian fashion, as the Dowager Countess's butler in the first series, as a general visiting the house with the Chief of Staff ('I gave myself a military cross because I was such a coward in the army in real life!') in the second, as a ghillie in Scotland, resplendent with a long beard, in the final episode of the third series and as the Lord Chamberlain announcing the debs at court in the fourth. Whatever his role in the fifth series – yet to be decided at the time of writing – we can be sure that Alastair Bruce will play it exactly right, down to the last stitch.

Alastair as a ghillie at the ball and (inset) as a decorated general.

SEPTEMBER

The House Party

Thomas
Barrow

SEPTEMBER

A house party is more than a highlight of the week at Downton Abbey – as we will see later, it has its very own raison d'être. A house party might consist of little more than two or three extra guests staying for a couple of nights, or it might be a rather more elaborate affair, with several important families and entertainment brought in to amuse, or it could centre around a shoot. But whatever the size, for the servants, the pace of life kicks up a gear as preparations begin.

C arson comes into his element as he prepares the wines and checks the silver. Mrs Hughes is never less than completely efficient, but in the days before guests arrive, she excels herself as she monitors the linens, runs a finger where the housemaids should have dusted and ensures the bedrooms are freshly made up. Mrs Patmore will be more hot and bothered than usual, running through the menus with Lady Grantham and snapping at Daisy. Cora, Mary, Edith and Rose all look forward to an excuse to wear their latest fashionable evening dresses and endless discussions will be had about the placement and which guest should sleep in which bedroom. With any luck, there will be a little romantic intrigue, though this will of course be confined to the drawing room. Robert just craves some decent conversation after dinner and Tom hopes not to feel like a fish out of water.

Aristocratic families across the country held power partly because they were the principal employers of the local area, owned the land that the farmers rented and were the focus of the village's entertainments. A peer would automatically have a seat in the House of Lords (today, hereditary peers must be elected in) and if he was ambitious – and most especially if his wife was – he would invite the influential people of the day to his house. In this way, he might gain further social and political influence, whether in arranging suitable marriages, conspiring against other politicians or simply running the country – members of the Cabinet might informally gather in someone's house and decide pressing matters there, rather than at 10 Downing Street.

In the days before trains and motorcars, house parties would last several days and guests would not always know their host all that well. The reputation of the family and the house would influence whether or not an invitation was accepted. For this reason, the work the servants did was immensely important: a house that was known to be efficiently run, with excellent food and wine, good service, comfortable beds, decent sport and so on was more likely to attract the movers and the shakers.

Robert and Cora are not wildly ambitious, but they have, in their time, been keen to see their daughters marry well and Robert has no objection to appearing distinguished and munificent before the county's families. Cora, as an American heiress to a retail fortune, is more bourgeois in her values; while she enjoys a good party and would like her guests to appreciate her giving one, she does not strike me as a person who would see any integrity in building a powerful reputation based on little more than being a sparkling hostess. Elizabeth McGovern thinks her character has changed over the years, which affects her social behaviour: 'To an extent, she's absorbing the time she lives in. She feels slightly more empowered to have a different opinion and is more comfortable standing up for herself and having her own separate interests to Robert. It is less a life that is a total reflection of his. I don't think she's in any way part of the emancipation of women, but she can't help but absorb that.'

That said, she has always enjoyed hosting potential suitors for her daughters and she takes seriously charitable events such as the village fête, as would have been deemed right and proper by the likes of her mother-in-law. Violet and Cora are still not exactly friends, but as Elizabeth says: 'They have a lot of respect for each other – they're allies. They both want the same things for the family.'

The one thing Cora would not have been responsible for, that hostesses today feel the pressure of, is the interior decoration. Houses of the Downton Abbey sort did not change madly after the Victorian age (the Victorians were enthusiastic builders and there was usually rather a lot of knocking down and building up again), and certainly they would not follow any interior fashions. If a young couple inherited a house that was falling down a bit, they might try to do some restoration, but that was the limit. Helen, Lady Dashwood, was married to Sir John Dashwood when they inherited West Wycombe (used today to film the interiors of Rosamund's London house). It was almost falling down after the First World War and they set to putting some of the rooms back, but it was a long job. In the magnificent book *The Country House Remembered* by Merlin Waterson, Lady Dashwood recalled: 'On one occasion, it seemed to me that some of the busts in the colonnade were missing, and the man I was talking to about it said, "Oh, I expect they will be in the Bust Room, my lady." 'It was in the old wing – I'd lived in the house for fifteen years and I'd never known there was such a thing – in a bedroom, with a staircase leading out of it onto the second or third floor, and it was absolutely full of busts. Some of them were quite good.'

There were strict social barriers up until the 1920s and we should not be fooled into thinking that they were completely relaxed thereafter, far from it, but they were loosened up slightly. Elinor Glyn was a social-climbing novelist of the 1890s who received instruction from a countess friend of hers as to who could and could not be asked to one's house. Army and navy officers could be invited to lunch or dinner, as could diplomats and clergymen. The local vicar might be a regular guest at Sunday lunch or supper, as long as he possessed the key qualification of being a gentleman (many vicars were the younger sons of gentry, but some, of course, were not). Doctors and solicitors tended to be garden-party-only people; no lunch or dinner invitations could ever come their way – the point about garden parties being that you did not introduce people to each other.

'There seems to be a good deal of emotion being vented among the guests in the library. But then they are foreigners.'

MRS HUGHES

CORA: *'You will have her next to you at dinner, and you will like it!'*

ROBERT: *'But what do I say to her? What does one say to a singer?'*

As the 1920s drew on, it started to become more fashionable to invite people who may not have been aristocratic, but were certainly entertaining – movie stars, distinguished sportsmen, musicians and so on. Before the First World War, these kinds of people would have been, if not quite 'below stairs', then certainly more suitable for the garden than the dining room. Hence, Robert's bewilderment when he is instructed by Cora to place Dame Nellie Melba, whom he has paid to sing for the guests, on his right at the dinner table, rather than serve her a tray in her room as Carson suggests.

House-party snobbery may have relaxed enough to allow the invitation of non-gentry, but strict rules of precedence were still observed, both above and below stairs. The higher you were in the peerage – i.e. royalty, duke, earl, viscount and so on – the better the bedroom you were given and the better the place at the dining table (mimicked in the servants' hall). The grandest female guest would sit to the right of the host; the grandest male guest to the right of the hostess. This had the unfortunate consequence that the hostess of a house party could find herself next to Duke Boring night after night.

The younger generations of 1924 behaved quite differently, at least in London, as we know from seeing Rose dance her way around the nightclubs. She almost certainly would have been reading about the exploits of the Bright Young Things in the newspapers and their new fashion for the 'stunt' or 'freak' party, in which outlandish fancy-dress costumes would be worn – there was a peculiar mode for dressing up as babies at one point. There was no precedence in their groups; what mattered was how extravagant and wild a party was – the more, the better, of course… and there was a lot of drink being drunk.

If the BYTs ever showed up at a parent's house, a culture clash was inevitable. Arthur Ponsonby's daughter Elizabeth, cousin to Loelia, was a notorious BYT and he recorded his frustration with her friends in his diary, after she turned up at home one weekend with one contingent in tow, another following on the next day, arriving at 3 p.m.: 'They consisted of a girl who seemed to have been picked up very late at night off Piccadilly. A shiny cinema actor, a bogus Sicilian Duke and two other anaemic undistinguished looking young men. At 5 brandy was called for by the girls as the sherry which had been going on during the afternoon had given out. Owing to the weather some decided to stay the night in Haslemere. So M went to make arrangements, bringing back four more bottles. At this point my patience broke down…

MRS HUGHES: *'The world does not turn on the style of a dinner.'*

CARSON: *'My world does.'*

Whoever their guests, the onus was always on the host to be welcoming and generous. This could be taxing when people suddenly announced they'd like to drop in, a particular threat to a house such as Downton Abbey, which was miles from anywhere – it meant guests were liable to stay for more than one cup of tea. 'Do people think we're a public house on the Great North Road?' complains Robert. Still, he would be on his best behaviour, because that was What One Did.

Julian tells a great story about his parents, forced into having a couple to stay at the end of the war: 'They came for a week and they stayed. And stayed. And stayed. And then at last it was time to say goodbye, a moment which, by some miracle, had been reached without the smiles ever cracking. The door shut with a click and my parents raced upstairs to celebrate. My mother leaped onto a table and started to dance a flamenco, swishing her skirts and petticoats to and fro, while my father circled below her, stamping his heels, clapping, whistling and laughing with glee. "They've gone!" they shouted, "They've gone!" Then they stopped. The guests were standing in the drawing-room door. "We forgot to leave our key," they said.'

While Robert might pay the bills, it is Mrs Patmore, Carson and Mrs Hughes who have to quickly accommodate unexpected guests. Menus have to be drawn up and extra food has to be ordered in. Bedrooms have to be given a polish, the beds quickly made up with fresh linen, a small vase of flowers arranged, clean towels laid out, and possibly Anna or Bates will have to double up their duties if the guest has no lady's maid or valet of their own. Robert and Cora are good employers, who are aware of the extra work put upon their servants. They also know that their servants' skills make the difference between a party going well and going badly, and Carson feels this pressure to a degree that can at times seem rather disproportionate. Thankfully, Mrs Hughes is usually on hand to put him right.

Molesley

Sarah Bunting at Downton Abbey.

EDITH: *'We ought to head off.*
If we're to be back before the gong.'

SARAH: *'The Rule of the Gong.*
It sounds like life in a religious order.'

Before the advent of the 'weekend', a new concept to the likes of Violet, who has little understanding of finishing work on a Friday and returning to it on Monday morning, the pinnacle of the 'Saturday-to-Monday' house party (as it was then known) was the Saturday night dinner, as guests arrived on Friday and left on Tuesday. As usual, the servants at Downton Abbey have a break for tea before Carson sounds the dressing gong – this signals the preparations for the evening. Mrs Patmore and her kitchen staff will attend to the final touches for the dinner, the footmen will lay the table in the dining room and Baxter, Anna, the silent Madge and Bates attend to their mistresses and master to help them change.

Clothes matter, particularly when Granny's coming for dinner. Violet's presence demands white tie, but perhaps now that the family do not dress up in white tie every night, they enjoy it rather more when they do. Mary, as a married woman, can wear a tiara to dinner; Edith and Rose will wear fashionable headpieces instead.

Baxter

Anna Robbins enjoys dressing Elizabeth McGovern as Cora: 'She's really stylish – she has a different take on it, as an American, and real flair. There's a soft fluidity to her look – things drape really well on her. I found some beautiful lace in Paris that was crying out for Elizabeth's frame. Her colours are muted and softer – rose, taupe – those work for her, as well as some dark reds and blues. You can really punch in with accents when you need to.'

Of course, no real lady gets ready alone – she needs the skills of her lady's maid to make her look the very best of herself. Since the departure of Cora's long-term lady's maid, the wicked Miss O'Brien, her replacement, Baxter, has been rather intriguing to follow. Her background has remained opaque and rather confusing – she seems nice, but if she is, how can she be in cahoots with the manipulative Thomas? Raquel Cassidy (Baxter), joining the show in series four, felt the same way as her character, walking into a house that already had established colleagues within it: 'She's nervous and wants to do a good job – and I was nervous and wanted to do a good job! If you look at the first few scenes, she's very happy and loves her work and soon becomes intensely loyal to Lady Grantham.' Baxter's best skill is as a seamstress: 'She's run up a couple of nice dresses for herself and I happen to really like them.' But, times being what they are, even a lady's maid may be called on to help out unexpectedly: 'We filmed a cocktail party and Baxter and some of the ladies from below stairs were handing out canapés. I don't do these scenes very often, but I enjoy it because it feels like training, with Alastair [Bruce] instructing.' Raquel quickly learned the importance of her character's work: 'One of the things to keep in mind is that they do have some downtime, but for the most part, they've got things on their mind and things to do; they get on with it with a certain sense of urgency. It's not emotion that drives their lives – that's almost secondary.'

Guests who have arrived from further afield may need to be introduced to each other. A book of etiquette published around 1925 offers clarity on exactly how these introductions should be received. When meeting guests at a dinner party or ball, parties should bow, but not shake hands. However, if you are meeting, say, the relations of your fiancé, then you must shake hands: 'These are assumed to be the beginnings of lifelong friendships, and so are inaugurated with more of heartiness and less of formality.' If a hand is offered, it should always be accepted, but one's handshake must be carefully devised: 'We all know the "pump-handle" shake, and the "concertina" shake, and the "piston shake" needs no description… All extremes are vulgar and society generally adopts the middle course.'

ROSE
'I love cocktail parties.'

CORA
*'Me too. You only have
to stay forty minutes,
instead of sitting
through seven courses,
stuck between a deaf
landowner and an even
deafer major general.'*

COCKTAILS

The Weekend Book, of which many editions were published, provided hosts with ideas for entertainment. The 1924 edition prints the lyrics of songs and poems and gives instructions for drawing-room games, cocktail recipes and even first-aid advice.

COCKTAIL RECIPES

Mr Sutton's Gin-Blind (to be drunk with discretion): Six parts gin, three parts Curaçao, two parts brandy and a dash of orange bitters.

Side-Car: Equal parts of fresh lemon juice (no alternative), Cointreau (or one of the orange liqueurs) and brandy.

Hawaiian: Four parts gin, two parts orange juice and one part Curaçao (or any other of the orange liqueurs).

In fashionable houses – of which Downton Abbey is *not* one – cocktails are served before dinner. This is a trend that began in London after the First World War, but moved very slowly around the counties. 'Not at Downton, I'm afraid,' apologises Mary to a guest who wonders where the pre-dinner drinks are. 'It may take another war.'

Instead, at Downton, strict etiquette is observed. Each man is assigned a woman to take through to supper. If a woman gets up from the table, all the men present stand. During the first course, the hostess will talk to the person on either her left or right, whichever direction it is, the rest of the women follow; for the main course, they 'turn' and talk to the person on their other side. Finally, at the end of the supper, the table 'splits', with the women getting up to have their coffee in the drawing room, while the men remain at the table with the port.

'Nothing is simpler than avoiding people you don't like. Avoiding one's friends is the real test.'

VIOLET, DOWAGER COUNTESS OF GRANTHAM

As hostess, Cora would definitely be judged on the food coming from her kitchens, despite the fact that she would not have been expected by anybody to have stirred a single sauce, let alone chopped an onion. She would, however, have planned the menu with Mrs Patmore and be well versed in the fashionable dishes and ingredients of the day. Likewise, Robert would be judged on the quality of the wine, although it is Carson who manages the cellar and would have, in all probability, selected the wines for the supper, with Robert merely nodding in agreement.

A grand dinner with guests from outside the family would have at least nine courses, each one modest in size ('I'll punish them,' said one cook of the 1920s, cross with her employer. 'I'll only serve six courses.'). Duff Cooper, a man who always seemed to be somewhere within the most influential social and political circles of his time, describes, in his 1924 diary, a dinner party he gave for four male friends: 'I took trouble about it and it was a great success. We had caviare, turtle soup, homard new burg [*Sic*] [a lobster dish], perdrix aux choux [partridge with cabbage], asparagus (which cost £1 a bundle), blackberry ice, mushrooms, sherry, Mumm 1911, light port, 1875 brandy. They all enjoyed it and praised the fare which certainly was damned good.' Note the use of French for the dishes, which was entirely in keeping, as well as the delight of the extravagant, out-of-season asparagus. The 'mushrooms' were almost certainly a savoury, an old-fashioned finish to a meal that meant one had a non-sweet taste in the mouth, allowing further drinking to ensue. Julian is on a campaign to bring back savouries and puts them into the script wherever possible.

After dinner is over, bar a glass of brandy and a cigarette (we don't see people smoking in *Downton* nearly as much as they would – it's one instance where modern sensibilities have to overrule historical accuracy, but in 1924 four in five men smoked and half the women; the smoke hung permanently in the air), the guests would go to bed. Cora and Robert are a rather romantic exception to the general rule that married couples slept in separate beds. In a very grand house, such as Downton, married couples would be given two bedrooms next door to each other, which gave them the choice of sleeping either together or separately. Similarly, in smaller houses, married guests would be given just the one bedroom, but with a dressing room next door, with a single bed made up in it.

Unmarried guests would be given bedrooms in either the female or bachelor corridors. This naturally meant that those who fancied a little 'corridor creeping', to steal into a fellow guest's bed, had the perfect opportunity. Lady Warwick famously had a bell rung at 6 a.m. at Easton Lodge, so everyone could get back to their own beds before the maids came in. Duff Cooper describes sneaking to a lover's room at 2 a.m. while his wife is away – 'a very long, dangerous and difficult journey in the dark over loud creaking boards and round a dozen corners'. There must have been several occasions when one *amour impropre* bumped into another as they felt their way down the gloomy hallways. But my favourite story, which did the rounds at the time, is of the man who leapt on his lover's bed in the dark, shouting, 'Cock-a-doodle-doo!' only to find he had awoken a bishop and his wife.

> *'Principles are like prayers. Noble, of course, but awkward at a party.'*
>
> VIOLET

It's exactly those awkward moments that Julian likes exploring – a house party is the perfect setting for him. 'What's interesting about a tight society is the moment when they get bored of doing everything correctly,' he explains. 'The exact moment when the rules are relaxed – that's interesting. With the Victorians, for example, it was all about the look of the thing. No one blamed you for being unhappily married or even having an affair, so long as you were discreet. But heaven help you if you started making a splash.'

Next morning, proprieties re-gathered, the married women would stay in bed to receive their breakfast on a tray from their lady's maids: a boiled egg and a cup of tea, perhaps. Baxter wins her American mistress's favour with a glass of freshly squeezed orange juice. The rest of the family and guests, the men and unmarried women, would have their first repast of the day in the dining room. The footmen would have served them the night before, but for breakfast, they merely fetch and carry the hot drinks, bacon, eggs and toast from the kitchens to the sideboard in the dining room; it is *de rigueur* for the guests to help themselves.

As series five progresses, we see Cora's character develop yet further. Elizabeth enthuses: 'We're getting to know who Cora is a lot more and I'm loving that she has much more of a distinct personality – there's a separate storyline that I'm absolutely relishing.' Few actors are with their characters for five years, as many of the *Downton* actors have been, and while there may be challenges in that, it brings its own rewards, as Elizabeth explains: 'You have to give it a variety of pacing, because you're fitting into a giant tapestry. It's been interesting to reconcile that. But I've absolutely loved the opportunity to live with a character so long; there's so much that's already there when you come to the table.'

Perhaps the greatest tribute to the show is that, in the end, the actors and crew working on *Downton Abbey* have the feeling of being at a long house party themselves – there is a lot of preparation to be done and crucial skills are needed to execute it successfully, but the end result is a good time had by all.

Simon
Bricker

PARMESAN STRAWS

These irresistible biscuits were a popular savoury (the final course after pudding, which has sadly now fallen out of fashion). They can also be presented as canapés to go with drinks in the more contemporary style.

MAKES ABOUT 25

100g Parmesan
100g plain flour,
  plus extra for dusting
a pinch of salt
a pinch of cayenne pepper
50g butter, plus extra
  for greasing
1 egg yolk

Preheat the oven to 200°C/400°F/gas 6. Lightly grease a large baking sheet.

Grate 75g of the cheese into a mixing bowl. Sift in the flour and add the salt and cayenne pepper. Crumble in the butter and rub in with your fingertips until you have a breadcrumb texture. Stir in the egg yolk and form the dough into a ball with your hands.

Dust the worktop and a rolling pin with a little flour. Roll the dough out in a rough square, to a thickness of about 5mm. Cut into strips about 1cm wide and 10cm long and gently transfer to the baking sheet. Finely grate the remaining Parmesan over the top of the straws.

Bake in the oven for 10–15 minutes until golden. Transfer to a wire rack to cool.

CHOCOLATE SOUFFLES

These soufflés would make an impressive dinner-party finale for the Crawleys –
take them straight to the table while they are at their full height.
Serve with double cream or vanilla ice cream.

SERVES 6–8

butter, for greasing
1 tablespoon cocoa powder,
    mixed with 1 tablespoon
    caster sugar, for dusting
100g dark chocolate,
    broken into pieces
2 tablespoons rum, brandy
    or espresso (optional)
4 egg yolks, beaten
6 egg whites
50g caster sugar
icing sugar, for dusting

Preheat the oven to 200°C/400°F/gas 6.

Grease several ramekins with butter, not forgetting the rims, then dust with the cocoa powder and caster sugar. Place on a baking tray.

Place the chocolate in a heatproof bowl set over a pan of barely simmering water. Make sure that the bottom of the bowl does not touch the water. Stir occasionally until the chocolate has melted. Take the pan off the heat and stir in the alcohol or coffee, if using. Allow to cool slightly, then stir in the beaten egg yolks.

Place the egg whites in a large bowl and beat with an electric mixer until soft peaks have formed. Add the sugar in stages, beating after each addition, until you have a thick, glossy consistency.

Very gently fold the chocolate mixture into the egg whites until the two are just incorporated. Divide the mixture between the ramekins. Bake in the oven for 8–10 minutes until risen. Dust with icing sugar and serve immediately.

SPOTLIGHT ON

EALING STUDIOS

All of the below-stairs scenes in *Downton Abbey*, as well as some of those that take place above stairs – the family's bedrooms, Robert's dressing room, the servants' attic bedrooms – are shot at Ealing Studios. The original site was developed in 1902, and has been used for film- and television-making ever since, as home to the Ealing comedies (from *Kind Hearts and Coronets* to *The Ladykillers*), but also other British hits, such as *Notting Hill* and the revived St Trinian's franchise.

Unlike the rarefied and chilly atmosphere of Highclere Castle, Ealing Studios is a busy, working film studios, which also houses the series' production offices along with the art, props, wardrobe, hair and make-up departments. The entrance is surprisingly low-key – a Portakabin with a few security guards sits at the front of a packed car park dominated by the caterers' lorry, as well as the trailers for costume, hair and make-up and the mobile production office – a.k.a. 'the AD truck' – which houses the second assistant director's office. The second AD is in charge of the logistics for the filming, liaising with all the departments to ensure that actors know where they need to be and when, as well as casting extras and looking ahead to take care of anything coming up such as booking a horse that is needed in two days' time.

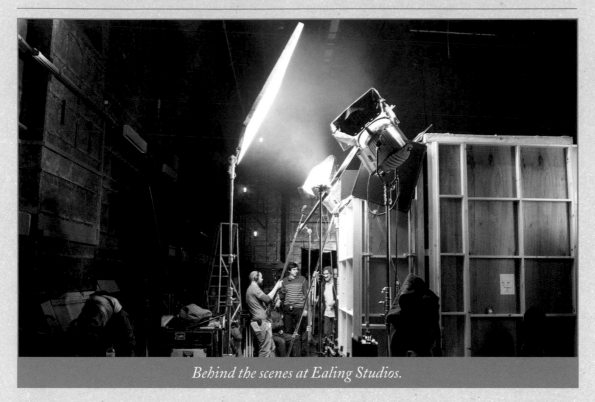

Behind the scenes at Ealing Studios.

The actors' dressing rooms – un-fancy affairs, with maybe a comfortable sofa or two, a coffee table and a mirror with the traditional light-bulb surround – sit inside the original white-painted brick buildings which contain the stages, their character names pinned on to the door.

The classic truism about being on a film set is that everyone is always in the way of someone else: with as many as eighty or ninety crew around on any given shooting day, each of whom has a specified and important job to do, it can be hard not to be obscuring someone's vision or path, as they all dodge around the edges of the enormous set walls.

On set, the beauty of *Downton Abbey* the show is somewhat hard to find at first. A tangle of wires, metal slats and hanging chains obscure the ceiling. The walls are lined with chicken wire, silver duct pipes and switches; the floors are worn-out laminate wood – to dampen the sound of people's footsteps. Along the side, you'll occasionally come across a trestle table with a vat of boiling water, boxes of tea and coffee sachets, polystyrene cups, some fruit – slices of watermelon, perhaps – and a tin or two of

variety biscuits (the Bourbons are always the first to go). You have to walk carefully, watching out for thick black cables snaking across the floor or metal light stands – while I was there, someone was nursing a sore head from walking into a wayward pole. The plywood backs of the set tell small tales, such as 'Mrs Hughes Sitting Room 5'.

While a scene is being shot, the footage from two cameras – 'Red' and 'Blue' – is shown on two monitors, sitting side by side on what appears to be a hostess trolley. Shabby directors' chairs – the kind you buy for garden picnics, with green nylon webbing and aluminium frames – are set in front, a small handmade plywood box hooked on to one arm to hold the owners' headsets: 'The Oracle' (as Alastair Bruce is reverently known), 'Good Queen Liz' for Liz Trubridge and 'Chris Croucher: the Lord Croucher of Downton Rushes' (his real title is 'producer'). Stuck on to the front of the trolley is today's lunch menu for cast and crew: 'Thurs 6 March 2014, Roast Rump of Lamb with a Mint and Redcurrant Jus, with New Potatoes, Carrots, Peas, Savoy Cabbage, followed by Jam Roly-Poly with Custard.' Suitably Downtonian, I think.

There's a hush that falls just before filming begins. The first AD is heard to shout: 'Stand by, nice and quiet please!' The take number is called and then: 'Action!' The same scene will be filmed from different angles and several takes will be shot. The number of angles, Chris Croucher explains, is to do with the eyelines – if one character looks at another, you need to film each actor for the reactions. If there's a conversation going on around the servants' hall, this can mean as many as twenty-five angles being shot. Retakes may also happen because Alastair Bruce requests that someone in the background is seen 'walking swiftly' rather than 'running' (no one ran indoors in 1924). One day's filming should produce around four or five minutes of film – it takes around twenty-six shooting days for two episodes in a 'block' to be completed, although this does not, of course, include the time needed for pre- and post-production business. The first and final longer episodes take around thirty-one days in total to shoot.

The evening before a day's filming, cast and crew are sent the day's call-sheet, detailing everything they need to know, from unit call time (the hour they have to be on set, usually 8 a.m., but if on location on, say, a London street, it can be a lot earlier) and wrap time (usually 7 p.m.), to the weather forecast. Scenes to be filmed are listed, with, for the casual visitor to the set, tantalising summaries: 'Breakfast. Thomas has a letter. Carson tells Bates to look after Lord G.' Extras needed are noted: '1 x House Maids; 2 x Hall Boys; 2 x Kitchen Maids'. Chris tells me they try hard to keep the same actors for non-speaking parts as far as possible, so that there is continuity, even in those unspoken, background narratives: 'Madge, who is referred to occasionally but has never spoken, has been the housemaid that dresses Edith since Anna became Mary's lady's maid. We only replace the hall boys when they start to look too adult for the part [they would have been about fourteen or fifteen years old]. It's nice to have the regulars – they know everyone and how it works. It's like bringing the family back together.'

Special effects that will be needed next day are noted too – smoke and steam in the kitchen, for example, or a fire in the library's hearth. The call-sheets are a good reminder as to how every single tiny detail that is seen on the screen has to be anticipated, planned and have a member of the crew take responsibility for it, in order for it to happen exactly as and when it is required. Which is pretty much how Carson and Mrs Hughes would run the house.

Allen Leech waits to go on set.

OCTOBER

Living on the Estate

OCTOBER

Living on the Estate

OCTOBER

We know that Downton Abbey is the home of the Earl of Grantham and his family, but it also provides a home, work and shelter for many others. A mere fifty years or so before, Downton Abbey would have had the same significance in its local area as Buckingham Palace does in London today.

The lord and lady of the manor were the small principality's own royalty, and their celebrations – weddings, and so on – were commemorated by everyone in the manor's village (as we saw on Lady Mary's wedding day in series three).

The best illustration of this is Consuelo Vanderbilt's description of her arrival at Blenheim in 1895. Consuelo was an extraordinarily rich American heiress who was more or less married off to the Duke of Marlborough by her ambitious mother, Alva. It was a famously unhappy marriage (they eventually divorced in 1921, having separated many years before), although her money arguably saved Blenheim Palace and made it the glorious house we enjoy today. Despite her having grown up in some of the biggest and most elaborate residences in New York and Newport, as well as enjoying a certain celebrity status on her side of the pond – a crowd of thousands pushed their way down Fifth Avenue to catch a glimpse of her on her way to her wedding – Consuelo was taken aback by the scale of the welcome designed especially for the Duke's bride.

Firstly, a private train took them to Woodstock from Oxford (a journey of seven miles); when they arrived at their station, there was a red carpet on the platform, upon which stood the Mayor in his scarlet robes, waiting to greet them with a speech. Instead of horses pulling their carriage to the house, a number of men did so, walking slowly through assembled crowds: 'Somewhat discomfited by this means of progress, at which my democratic principles rebelled, I nevertheless managed to play the role in fitting manner, bowing and smiling in response to the plaudits of the assembled crowds,' wrote Consuelo in her memoir, *The Glitter and the Gold*. 'Triumphal arches had been erected, children were waving flags, the whole countryside had turned out to greet us and I felt deeply touched by the warmth of their welcome.'

This kind of focus on the aristocratic families was partly because people travelled very little then (train travel was still quite expensive and only really used for special trips by the working classes), so their entire lives were centred on the small area in which they lived, and partly because 'the big house', as it was invariably known, was the primary source of employment. This is the great responsibility that Robert feels: to ensure that the house keeps going in order that it may continue to serve the local populace in the way that it always has, as well as keeping his family in a seat of power. Traditionally, this was easily done – an estate that had enough land to lease to tenant farmers needed only to collect the rents in order to pay for the running of the estate.

By the time Mary starts shouldering some of this responsibility, things have changed. Taxation is much higher (the standard income tax rate in 1914 was 6 per cent; in 1918, 30 per cent), agricultural depressions have left many farmers unable to pay their rent and the cost of servants and labourers is much higher. There is less money to go around and it's harder to squeeze it out of the tenants – there has to be a new way forward if the estate is to survive.

Mary's priorities are, then, slightly different from her father's – her primary concern is that the house and estate are kept whole, so that her son may inherit. To this end, if there is a tenant who cannot pay, she would rather he was evicted and another found who can, rather than – as is Robert's inclination, and as we saw with the Drewe family – allowing them to stay for no other reason than it has always been their home.

Cottages on the estate were not always rented out (hence not every inch of the land was making money for the landowner) – many were given to retired servants, as well as a few to those who were married but working for the house, as with Anna and John Bates. Many more were given to workers on the estate – married ones would be given their own, unmarried workers might have to bunk up together. These were often rated as prime positions, not just because the employee was given both work and a place to live, but because there would be 'pickings', whether that was a rabbit or two from a generous gamekeeper or a stray bit of game for the pot.

Mr and Mrs Bates decorate their cottage on the estate.

BROWN
SODA BREAD

*Soda bread is traditionally made in northern England, Scotland and Ireland.
It uses bicarbonate of soda as the raising agent, which is activated by the acidity
of the soured milk. Soda bread is very quick and easy to make
and is best eaten warm, the day it is baked.*

MAKES 1 LARGE LOAF

450ml buttermilk
 or 350ml full-fat milk
 and juice of ½ lemon
275g plain white flour,
 plus extra for dusting
275g wholemeal flour
1 rounded teaspoon
 bicarbonate of soda

Preheat the oven to 230°C/450°F/gas 8. Dust a baking sheet with flour.

If using full-fat milk, pour it into a large jug, add the lemon juice and leave to stand for about 15 minutes at room temperature, by which time it will have thickened and curdled slightly.

Sieve the flours and bicarbonate of soda into a large bowl. Add the bran left in the sieve from the wholemeal flour. Stir well. Make a well in the centre and gradually add the buttermilk or soured milk, using your hand as a claw to mix it in. Using your hands, bring the dough together, but do not knead it. The dough should be soft but not sticky. If it's too wet, add a little more flour.

Place the dough on the baking sheet and tidy into a round, tucking the edges underneath to give a smooth outline. Pat the top lightly to flatten it a little, then cut a deep cross in the top using a large knife. Dust with a little flour and bake in the oven for 15–20 minutes. Reduce the heat to 200°C/400°F/gas 6 and bake for a further 20–25 minutes, until the loaf has a good colour and sounds hollow when tapped on the underside. Leave to cool on a wire rack.

SLOE GIN

Sloes are the sour little fruit of the blackthorn tree and appear in the hedgerows in early autumn. Wild food like this would have been freely available to tenants of the estate. What better way to use sloes than to make this warming winter liqueur?

MAKES 1 LITRE

450g sloes
450g granulated sugar
1 litre bottle of gin

Wash and de-stalk the sloes. Spread them on a baking sheet in a single layer and freeze overnight.

Next day, pack the sloes into a large, sterilised glass bottle that has an airtight seal. Add the sugar, using a funnel. Pour in the gin until the bottle is full. Screw the lid on tightly and give the bottle a good shake.

Shake the bottle once a day over the next week to help the sugar disperse and dissolve, and then shake it once a week until Christmas, by which time it should be ready to drink. The gin will continue to mature in the bottle for 1–2 years, so if you can keep it for longer, so much the better!

The sloe gin is best drunk neat, but it can be topped up with tonic water or mixed into a cocktail.

NOTE

The gin-soaked sloes that remain in the bottle can be made into a delicious chocolate bar. Line a baking tray with greaseproof paper. Stone the fruit and spread out on the paper, along with some lightly toasted hazelnuts. Gently melt some dark or milk chocolate and pour over in an even layer. Leave to set.

Unfortunately, as these cottages brought no money in for the family, they were often not terribly well kept up and were frequently damp and dark – there was no national grid until 1938, so they had no electricity either. We see Anna and Bates (will she ever call her husband 'John'?) sitting in their cottage with oil lamps. The cottages did at least give the workers some privacy and they enabled the landlord to save old retired servants from the workhouse if they had no family or savings to prop up their remaining years. Although a great number of aristocratic families would have found it increasingly difficult to support their retired servants after the First World War, many blamed the Liberal Prime Minister Lloyd George's welfare benefits for their failure to do so – they claimed that compulsory contributions to employees' health insurance and pensions meant they couldn't afford to look after their servants in the way they might have ordinarily done.

The question of health and old age were serious for the worker with little provision beyond their basic wage. Those in the house might have access to the local doctor, but if there was no surgery to visit discreetly, he would have to attend to a patient in their room. Naturally, this meant that the entire household would know within a matter of minutes that a servant had been seen by a doctor, so many servants chose to treat themselves rather than become the subject of gossip.

Dr Clarkson

The health of the family and servants at Downton Abbey is managed by Dr Clarkson and, to a lesser extent, Isobel Crawley, as she had grown up in a medical family and been married to a doctor – she was certainly very involved with the local hospital when she arrived at Downton and later went to work for the Red Cross in France during the First World War. This was a time of great medical change and advance – we hear about the arrival of insulin in series five, for example – though many new treatments were felt to be too unproven and were not easily adopted by rural doctors. David Robb, who plays Dr Clarkson, admits his character is 'not cutting edge'. David believes Dr Clarkson is really in retirement: 'I think he was jilted badly, so never married, but went into the army as a medical doctor in the Boer War and has now retired as a GP in Yorkshire. He's not stupid, but he is a bit of a plodder. He is very honourable and does what he thinks is right – unfortunately, it isn't always.'

When Mrs Hughes is threatened with cancer (in series three), we see that it is a real worry as to what will happen to her if the diagnosis is positive. Fortunately, Cora is a sympathetic employer and is able to reassure her that she will be looked after as a long-standing member of the household. But Mrs Hughes knows she is lucky.

The art department created the workhouse location, capturing the gloom, poverty and hard labour of its inmates. Those without money or family support, such as single mothers, would live in fear of being sent to such a place.

The workhouses were frequently filled with former domestic servants, forced to see out their old age or terminal illnesses in squalid sanatoriums, minimally treated by doctors who had to rely on the haphazard and ill-educated assistance of other inmates. Before welfare benefits, workhouses were the only provision for people unable to earn enough money to keep a roof over their heads and meals on the table. As they were largely unregulated, it was sheer luck of the draw that saw an impoverished person land up at a workhouse that provided well for its residents.

In general, however, the poor were treated almost as a criminal class. The children were beaten for the slightest misdemeanours; families were separated, with the women in one area, the men in another and the children in yet another (they would be reunited for an hour on Sundays). The food was basic and mean, the work harsh – breaking stones for gravel or building materials was a common task. By the 1920s, workhouses were improving or gradually disappearing, due to better regulation and the growth of the welfare state, but for the older generation there was still a very real fear that they would die there. This was why Mrs Hughes feels such sympathy for Carson's former friend, Mr Grigg, when she hears he had ended up in a workhouse – for all his past sins, she believes it would be too hellish a condemnation for anyone.

As workers on the estate were frequently recruited from the local village, the house was at the centre of the area's entertainments and even political life, with the residing lord or lady often appointed chair of a board for, say, the school, hospital or even of a committee for erecting a monument, particularly after the First World War, when commemorations were established for the men who had died.

Village children in series five.

Anna Bates

With the house known to all, there was always the threat of the unwelcome intruder – and Mrs Hughes turns to this for an explanation as to how Anna is attacked the night Dame Nellie Melba comes to sing at Downton Abbey. It is an entirely believable alibi – the back door would almost never be locked.

The storyline was shocking, and so it should have been – as good as the old days might have been, there were terrible times too, and the series does not shy from them. Gareth Neame explains: 'We ask ourselves – what is the big story for this character? With this particular one, we felt with Anna and Bates that they had been through Bates-related stories that Anna had resolved. This time it was reversed, with Anna at the centre. Bates is generally melancholic and Anna supremely positive and we flipped that around. We're always putting roadblocks and obstacles in our characters' way.'

What was crucial for the production was how they handled this particular scene: 'Rape is depicted frequently on television,' says Gareth. 'We were not going to trivialise it. We also recognise that we cannot underestimate the degree to which these characters are loved. But it's part and parcel of what we do – because there's so much comedy and romance in the show, people forget that there's a tougher edge to it too. I like the way we deliver these stories. In that episode, the audience is led to believe the focus is on the house party with Dame Nellie Melba, when in fact what is really going on is below stairs. As the story unfolded, it was so brilliantly performed – it was ultimately about Anna and Bates's marriage – not to shock and surprise.'

Perhaps the biggest challenge was for the actress Joanne Froggatt (Anna Bates), who has seen her character develop hugely over the series. 'She's grown as a woman. She met Mr Bates, fell in love and then had to overcome trials and tribulations, as well as being involved in the day-to-day things of the house. I see her now as a little more knowing than in the first series. She's still got a lot of worries on her mind,' she says.

Of her character's own backstory, she has some ideas. 'You want to have some kind of background in your head, even if that's not the same as Julian's,' she laughs. 'In my head, Anna has grown up within the village boundaries, possibly in a farming family. I think she's very emotionally mature and possibly experienced death at a young age – perhaps she was the oldest of all the siblings and a mother figure to them. She's also got a strong work ethic and comes from a hardworking family. She's an old head on young shoulders.'

Joanne understands the attraction between Anna and Bates: 'When they first meet, they're both good people trying to stay on the right side of the moral line. They have strong ethics and a strong moral code, as well as being emotionally intelligent. They've come to the same stage at different ages and for different reasons, but they have that in common. Bates tries to be a good man and do the right thing – Anna admires that in him.'

The rape scene was not something Joanne approached lightly. 'I spoke to Gareth and the director and we had not so much a rehearsal as a discussion, working out how we'd shoot it, thinking about what it meant for Anna and Bates. I planned it with Nigel Harman [the actor playing Mr Green, her attacker] and planned the emotional journey. That was really helpful because of the subject matter – we needed to do that. I spoke too to Alastair [Bruce] about what it meant for a woman in those times. He explained that then a woman had no rights, only her reputation, her family and her career. If society found out what had happened to her, she would be in danger of losing all three, because people would say there was no smoke without fire. It sounds barbaric, but that's how it was. I understood the enormity of something like that happening, the political and social implications added on to what was already a horrific and terrifying experience.'

The biggest challenge in the filming was, for Joanne, to get it absolutely right: 'I like a challenge, but you certainly feel much more under pressure. Viewers might be watching it thinking of something like that having happened to them or to someone they knew – if they saw an actor doing it not very believably or not giving it their all, that would be hugely insulting and wrong. I knew I had to get it right.'

Fortunately, for someone like Anna, although she would not feel she could talk about what had happened to her, she would at least draw comfort from the close society around her. The servants below stairs were another kind of family, after all, and those living on the estate would have had the sense of being all together, part of the same community. They watched out for one another, helped and lent a hand when it was needed. In the end, they didn't have much – but they did have each other.

MUSIC

Hearing the rousing music for the *Downton Abbey* theme tune signals across the world that it's time to stop what you're doing, grab a cup of tea or glass of wine and settle down in front of the television for an hour or so, immersed in the world of the Crawley family. There must be an almost Pavlovian connection now between the *Downton* score and a sharp increase of serotonin in viewers from Buckingham to Boston.

The entire score for the show, since it first began, is the work of one man, composer John Lunn. John and Gareth Neame are old friends and long-term collaborators and, for Gareth, there was little question as to whom he would turn to for *Downton*: 'He is remarkably versatile and can do anything.' John's work includes scoring dramas such as *Bleak House* and *Little Dorrit* – Dickensian adaptations with modern scores. It is this approach that informed his new project. 'From the first episode, we couldn't ignore the fact that it was 1912, but we wanted a modern feel to it,' says John. 'I decided to keep the orchestration very clean – piano, strings, an occasional cor anglais (it's like an oboe, and very evocative of the English landscape), saxophone or vibraphone. It's an unusual combination, but all of those instruments were around then.' John explains that while Edwardian music is harmonically quite advanced, 'It is too overwrought to work as an underscore for a drama. I needed something much slower and clearer.'

Dame Kiri Te Kanawa as Dame Nellie Melba.

John is the last piece in the jigsaw puzzle, coming on board when the episode has been filmed and edited: 'As so much of the music is about the timing and linking scenes, we can't compose until that is absolutely set in stone. I usually have around two to two and a half weeks for my work on each episode. I had more time for the first, as that was absolutely key.'

The very first episode, in fact, did not feature the opening title and score with which we are now all so familiar, but began with John Bates sitting on the train. We followed him, looking rather nervous and apprehensive, and trailed the tracks of a telegram as it flew through the telegraph lines overhead, before arriving triumphantly at the magnificent Downton Abbey. 'I used just a solo piano tune for Bates, with a rising emotional string melody for the picture of the house,' says John. 'The next scene was watching the servants as they got up and got the house ready – we referenced the music and its energy from the train, almost showing another kind of well-oiled machine.' Having worked on this first episode, it informed the rest: 'By the time we'd finished it, it was clear to us what the music would be for the title. It was a real stroke of luck and I wish they all worked out like that! Even now, having done four series, we can still see the music stem from that very first episode.'

A few episodes have opened without the iconic titles for a variety of reasons – such as when the show returned after the shocking death of Matthew. 'There was a feeling that we couldn't go back as if nothing had happened, although time had passed,' says John. 'We used that opening episode of series four to establish how the rest of it would go – it was about the rehabilitation of Mary.' Twitter went berserk, with people believing the music they knew and loved had been ditched, but of course it returned for the next episode.

The fans of the show have taken the music to their hearts, as they have everything else. Much to his surprise, John has been told of heavy-metal versions of his score and 'There's even a ukulele version – you name it! [Comedian] Will Ferrell was skating to it in a sketch on *Saturday Night Live*. It's really taken on a life of its own.'

John has helped the fans along by recording two albums of *Downton* music, writing lyrics with Don Black ('Born Free', 'The Man with the Golden Gun'), the second of which reached No. 1 of the USA's classical music charts. The hit song on the album was inspired by the scene in series two when Mary rushes to the train station to say goodbye to Matthew and gives him her lucky stuffed dog. It happens to be one of Julian Fellowes's favourite scenes and, it turns out, John's too: 'I recently showed that scene to film students without the music and with the music, but as

I sat there, I realised that it's such a good scene, the music didn't actually make enough of a difference to prove my point!' None of the cast feature on the album, but given the skills of Elizabeth McGovern (who sings with her own band, Sadie & the Hotheads) and Michelle Dockery (an accomplished jazz singer), this seems a shame: 'I'll try to persuade them for the next one,' laughs John.

Series four portrayed the beginning of a very exciting new world for music. 'The whole of the twentieth century is really about black music – we wouldn't have pop music today without it and even avant garde classical music is defined by how it approaches that genre,' says John. There were technical challenges with the music of the jazz band as both background and storyline for some of the scenes: 'It's to do with the timing – you can't cut away from a song, wait for the line to be delivered and cut back. It was complicated in post-production. There seems to be less live music in series five…'

One other significant time that the music was featured was in series four, when Dame Nellie Melba – a cameo appearance by Dame Kiri Te Kanawa – came to sing for the guests at Cora and Robert's house party. John says the music chosen for the pivotal scene, when the guests are rapt listening to Melba sing, not knowing of the brutal attack on Anna taking place below stairs, was deliberately romantic, creating the juxtaposition of mood. The choice of music was ultimately made by Dame Kiri herself. She was given the choice of songs so long as it suited the situation and in the end, sang 'Mimi's Farewell', 'Songs My Mother Taught Me' and 'O Mio Babbino Caro'.

John is always thinking about what will happen in the musical world of *Downton:* 'When I'm working on it, I never turn the dialogue off and I'm always looking at the picture. Every tune is separately recorded, even if it sounds familiar – there's no manipulation. Hopefully, the music beneath the dialogue is what makes it work. It's about helping the storylines, and in a long-running series where people might miss an episode, the music is a shorthand to help them hear what it's about and understand the relationships between the characters.'

A musician tunes up.

NOVEMBER
The Sporting Season

NOVEMBER

The Earl of Grantham is the quintessential Englishman at home in his castle. It's not the comfort of his chair by the hearth that he seeks, nor even the pleasures of a glass of whisky after a delicious supper at his dining table. No, a man like Lord Grantham is truly at his happiest when the cold wind is whipping his face, the rain is pelting at his back, his tweed suit hangs heavy and his feet are worn out and aching from tramping up and down dale, a shotgun broken across his arm.

If there is anything that defines the aristocratic country gentleman, it's his love of outside activities, particularly those that both celebrate and take part in the countryside itself. While summer games, such as cricket and tennis, are much enjoyed, whether on the village green or one's own lawn, it's the country sports of winter that rouse the aristo's spirits with a single note from the bugle. A gentleman would hardly know whether he actually enjoyed hunting, shooting or fishing – he would have been brought up to enjoy it and would expect nothing less of himself, nor of those around him.

Arguably, as landowners began to travel to town more frequently for matters of business during the week, the pull of the country's attractions grew ever stronger. Lady Colin Campbell's book, *Etiquette of Good Society,* had a romantic view: 'What town-wearied man does not feel refreshed and reinvigorated as he climbs the hills with a gun on his shoulder and a dog at his heels? And for the time being is not his one wish – "Give me the naked heavens above. The broad bare heath below"?'

Lord Grantham is no exception. His estate affords him the ability to hold shooting parties for friends each winter and the drive of the house is large enough to act as the meeting place for the start of a day's hunt. Any friend who declines an invitation to join these events is invariably considered 'not quite a gentleman'.

Or even 'not quite a gentlewoman'. While women were not obliged to take part in the country sports, those who could, and who held their own against the men, were admired. In fact, hunting was seen as a growing activity for women – in 1922 there were twenty-five women hunters for every one there had been in 1880. We saw, in the very first season, Mary ride out with the hunt, as bravely and as fast as the rest of them, in side-saddle no less – her horsemanship, indeed, considered a central part of Kemal Pamuk's attraction to her.

I do wonder if it was the possibility of romance that made hunting so attractive to women after the war – men were scarce on the ground then, but a woman who rode out with a hunt would earn the respect of her fellow riders before changing into a beautiful dress for the hunt ball that night, dancing until the early hours. The perfect opportunity to meet an eligible young man.

All of the sports have their own seasons – shooting and fishing are in line with the times when the birds and fish are fully grown and plentiful; hunting is enjoyed when the fields are fallow, and therefore fine for riding roughshod over, the farmers are not too busy and landowners are seeking entertainment during the grey, cold days of an English winter.

Hunting, for many, is the most glamorous of the sports – riders in their scarlet coats (actually called 'Pink' because a Mr Pink used to make them) and white breeches, astride glossy steeds, the well-trained pack of hounds running in and out of the horses' legs, as the hunt meets in front of a beautiful house.

Hunting could be a family affair. Lavinia Smiley recalled riding out as a young girl with the Cowdray Hounds, of which her father was a joint master. Although she clearly found it thrilling when the hounds caught the scent of a fox, there was no denying that hunting could also be terrifically frightening: 'The hunting days were mostly filled with terror, both physical and social, and worst of all were days with the Crawley and Horsham, because they were often on the Downs, and once on the Downs and galloping there was no reason to suppose one would ever be able to stop. All my nightmares were of being Run Away With.' Lavinia took less pleasure in the trophies (a fox's paw) or the blooding (a rather gruesome tradition, in which a huntsman smeared a small amount of blood on a new rider's face, which you had to keep on for as long as possible) than the lunch: 'The best thing about hunting was your leather sandwich case, strapped on to the side of the saddle. Barley water in the bottle, and mutton sandwiches or toast and bacon in the silver tin. "Have you eaten yours yet?" "No, I'm SAVING it."'

The great changes to the agricultural landscape after the First World War had their effect on the sport too. A large number of new owner-occupiers tended to be less sympathetic than the old tenant farmers and wanted to be paid a fee for allowing the hunt to cross their fields.

Farmers were – and still are – more sympathetic to shoots, which often earned them a fee if they sold shooting days to syndicates on their land. More typically, a landowner would host shooting parties on his own land across the season – for friends before Christmas, then in January he would invite his tenants, although less for pheasant and woodcock than for rabbit, which ran wild on the estate.

A shoot began with a hearty breakfast, after which the host gave each 'gun' (which refers to the guest, not the weapon) a number, to assign them their 'peg' for the day. At each drive, the numbered pegs were stuck into the ground to show where each gun stood; he would stand there either alone or with his loader (a man to help load one gun while he shoots with the other) and possibly his own gun dog, who would retrieve his birds at the end of the drive.

Everyone would be taken out in one or two 'wagonettes' to the first drive, unless it was within walking distance. (In fact game shoots are run in exactly the same way today, one hundred years later, down to the long socks and plus-fours the guns wear.) There would be several drives in a day, each one slightly different in aspect, whether hill or open field, with beaters (farm hands, usually, employed for this particular task) urging the birds – mostly pheasant, raised especially for this purpose – to fly out where they would be in sight of the guns. The drives would last all morning, with stops for a shot of hot consommé, fortified with sherry, and maybe a sandwich.

THE SPORTING SEASONS

RED GROUSE: 12 AUGUST TO 10 DECEMBER
PARTRIDGE: 1 SEPTEMBER TO 1 FEBRUARY
PHEASANT: 1 OCTOBER TO 1 FEBRUARY
NO GAME MAY BE KILLED ON SUNDAYS OR CHRISTMAS DAY. NO SHOOTING AT NIGHT.
HUNTING AND POINT-TO-POINT SEASON OPENS 1 NOVEMBER

'I never know which is worse: the sorrow when you hit the bird, or the shame when you miss it.'

MARY

In 1924 shooting was a relatively new sport. Before the advent of the perfected shotgun and the systematic rearing of tame birds, a landowner walking his estate wouldn't expect to shoot more than ten birds in a day. The social historian David Cannadine writes that on one estate in Norfolk, only thirty-nine birds were killed in 1821; sixty years later, the figure was 5,363. As the sport increased in popularity, the number of birds killed could be vast. Lord de Grey was an exception among his peers, known to be the best shot of all, and his statistics are staggering. Between 1867 and 1923 he slaughtered 250,000 pheasant, 150,000 grouse and 100,000 partridge. Cannadine reports that there was one small punishment: 'After a day's sustained shooting, it was almost impossible to avoid suffering from a violent headache.'

Those women who did not shoot could find the whole affair rather tedious. Consuelo Vanderbilt, the American heiress unhappily married to the Duke of Marlborough, certainly did. In her memoir she writes of hours spent waiting around, with little to do but change in and out of outfits according to the time of day (she had sixteen dresses for one four-day house party). Occasionally they would stand by the guns for a drive or two – but this could be a damp and thankless task. More fun was the luncheon which allowed for much drinking and merriment to commence, despite the fact that there would be two or three more drives in the afternoon. Shooting lunches would be laid out in a barn rather than the main house, where muddy boots could be kept on but everything else would be as correct as usual, with the butler pouring the wine and the footmen serving.

Alastair Bruce's knowledge of shooting helped the *Downton* cast here. When the actors needed to learn how to handle a gun, a day was booked for them at a shooting school and, much to Alastair's delight, 'I was handed a gun and hit everything.' (Schools use clays, not game, by the way.) So on the day of the film 'shoot' itself, Alastair was cast as a guest of the shooting party.

'Maids at a shooting lunch – hardly.'
CARSON

ROAST GAME BIRDS

Roasting is the most delicious way to enjoy young game birds, whereas older birds are more suited to braising or casseroling. Be generous with the butter and add herbs and other flavourings of your choosing. You can also put some seasoned butter inside the carcass for pheasant, partridge, mallard, widgeon and teal.

A traditional way to serve game birds is to cut a piece of bread the size of each bird, toast lightly and spread with butter. About 10 minutes before the end of the birds' cooking time, slide a piece of toast under each bird, to soak up all the cooking juices. Serve the birds on the toast, with a pile of watercress and any other accompaniments of your choice.

APPROXIMATE COOKING TIMES

Grouse (one bird serves 2): roast for 30–40 minutes.

Pheasant (one hen pheasant serves 2; a cock serves 3): roast for 45–60 minutes (depending on size).

Partridge (one bird serves 1): roast for 20 minutes.

Snipe and woodcock (one bird serves 1): roast for 15–20 minutes.

Mallard (one bird serves 2): roast for 30–40 minutes.

Widgeon and teal (one bird serves 2): roast for 15–20 minutes.

Preheat the oven to 220°C/425°F/gas 7.

Using your hands, smear softened butter all over the birds and season generously with sea salt and freshly ground pepper.

Lay the birds on a roasting rack set in an oven tray. Roast for the time indicated left, basting occasionally and turning the birds over halfway through cooking.

Turn off the oven, leaving the door ajar, and leave the birds to rest for 10 minutes before serving.

The First World War was to have an unexpected effect on the sport, however. Hunting and shooting had been suspended during the war years and when it returned, there was an entirely different aspect to it in the minds of some. Cannadine puts it best in *The Decline and Fall of the British Aristocracy:* 'After so much slaughter on the Somme, even the mass extermination of birds seemed somehow distasteful.' Daisy Warwick wrote in her memoir, *Life's Ebb and Flow,* about her aversion to any kind of bloodsport after the war: 'I am not alone in this feeling. Men friends – themselves crack shots – have told me that although they formerly enjoyed the shooting season, they can no longer find pleasure in killing birds or ground game, from a new feeling of reluctance to take life of any kind.'

Cannadine believes it was really only King George V's enthusiasm for the sport, which his country hosts at Welbeck, Elveden, Holkham or Chatsworth would feel obliged to arrange, that allowed it to continue in the Edwardian manner. (George V's father, King Edward VII, famously enjoyed shooting parties, but although he certainly shot a lot of birds, I think he enjoyed the party side of things as much, if not more. King George V just wanted to shoot down as many birds as he possibly could.) The farmer A. G. Street saw it somewhat differently: he recalled a 'heavy weight' lifting from the population at the end of the war, which sent everyone 'pleasure mad'. As he wrote his memoir, looking back from the vantage point of the Depression, he must have felt as if those years after the war were especially indulgent. He calls it 'a tawdry life' – in which farmers swanked in motor cars, swapped their breeches for plus-fours and a blue suit for a dinner jacket. But it seems entirely understandable that after all the grief and tragedy, many men and women would seek to make the most of what could be a very short life.

Each sport brought its own set of rules, from dress to conduct. Each hunt would have its own costume, but these tended not to vary too greatly from either a scarlet or dark-green coat. These would be worn with white knee-breeches, top-boots, a tall hat or black velvet cap with a stiff peak, spurs, of course, and a stylish cashmere scarf, fastened by a pin. Women would wear a tight-fitting habit, made with a sort of apron skirt over breeches (they were largely riding astride rather than side-saddle by 1924). They would often wear a high hat with a short veil, with other elegant accessories – gloves, a whip. They did not wear scarlet jackets, although some might have a scarlet waistcoat. For shooting, men wore heavy tweed plus-fours (trousers that end just below the knee) and jackets, with long socks and walking boots, together with a flat cap. Although women were not shooting, they would dress almost as if they were, with a skirt and jacket in tweed too.

Evelyn
Napier

Returning home, sportsmen and women would often be filthy from the splattered mud of the fields. This was a particular problem with hunting and it was down the poor valet to deal with it. Ernest King, in his memoir *The Green Baize Door*, had an unusual, if effective, method: 'From horse and rider perspiring, from a fall in a muddy ditch or field, they can come back in a pretty mess, especially the coat tails. When in this state we would ask the housemaid to save us the contents of the chamber-pots, at least a bucketful. It was truly miraculous in getting the dirt out. That was immediately followed, I hasten to add, by brushing with clean water. I've often wondered if all the smart and fashionable hunting folk ever knew of the means taken to keep their coats so smartly turned out.'

A MORE PLEASANT METHOD TO CLEAN A HUNTING COAT

FROM GENTLEMEN'S GENTLEMEN (1976)

'If a coat came back filthy dirty I'd put it on a clothes hanger with two largish stones in the pockets, plunge it into a rain-water butt, leave it to soak for a couple of minutes, then hang it above the butt and brush it down with a large dandy brush. The process would be repeated several times until the dirt was completely removed and the water was running away clean from the jacket. I'd then remove the stones, hang it outside until it had drained sufficiently, and put it in the drying room where it would drip and slowly dry. It had to be examined every so often because if it became the slightest bit creased it would stay like it for ever… White breeches I would wash in Lux soapflakes.'

YORKSHIRE PARKIN

Variations on this oaty gingerbread are traditionally enjoyed in Yorkshire – Downton Abbey's own county – on Bonfire Night. Keep it in a tin for a few days before cutting and eating.

MAKES ONE 20CM SQUARE CAKE

450g plain flour
a pinch of salt
1 teaspoon bicarbonate
    of soda
2 teaspoons ground ginger
1 teaspoon mixed spice
350g porridge oats
225g butter, plus extra
    for greasing
225g soft brown sugar
225g black treacle or golden
    syrup, or a mixture
3 large eggs

Preheat the oven to 160°C/325°F/gas 3. Grease a deep 20cm square cake tin and line the base with greaseproof paper.

Sieve the flour, salt, bicarbonate of soda, ginger, mixed spice and baking powder into a large mixing bowl, then stir in the oatmeal.

Place the butter, sugar and treacle in a small pan and gently heat until melted, then add to the bowl. Stir well to combine.

Break the eggs into a bowl, beat well and then stir into the mixture.

Spoon into the prepared cake tin and smooth the top. Bake in the oven for 50–60 minutes, or until a skewer inserted in the middle comes out clean. Take care not to overcook the cake or it will be dry.

Cool the cake in the tin, and when completely cold, remove, wrap well and store in an airtight tin.

Mary's bewitched suitor, Tony Gillingham, whom we meet for the first time in series four, fits into this world perfectly; brought up a gentleman, he would hunt, shoot and fish with aplomb. The actor playing him, Tom Cullen, enjoyed learning the rules and etiquette for a young man in 1924, from taking his hands out of his pockets, to not slouching and getting in the saddle. Even the clothes were a part of this: 'It was the first time I'd ever had a suit made for me and I know Julian and Alastair spent ages selecting a beautiful country fabric. It makes you feel like a completely different person. It wasn't until I started to wear the costume that I had an educated idea about how he walked and held himself.'

The challenge for Tom was establishing his character when everyone else had been there for some time before: 'I wanted to make sure he was someone you felt existed outside the house,' he explains. 'The parallels are interesting, with him and Mary both taking on their estates. His father has died recently and he's struggling with the enormity of the task before him.' Despite his upbringing, Tom believes Tony is uncomfortable with the life he's in: 'He's inherently quite a sad man, trapped in a system he no longer believes in. You get the feeling he's hiding away and when he meets Mary, she makes him feel alive, that maybe he does have a chance to live a life that he might actually want. She gives him vitality.' Because there is such a large cast of characters on this show, the actors face a challenge, but one that excites them, as Tom explains: 'It's like a tapestry – you have to make a lot of your own choices, but that's something Julian wants.'

For this reason, Tom developed a whole backstory for Tony, beginning with sitting down with Alastair Bruce and tracing his character's possible lineage in *Burke's Peerage* (the definitive guide to genealogy, lineage and heraldry, from peerage to landed gentry; it's been in use since 1826): 'We know he's a viscount, so that helped. I decided he was one of three brothers and two of them have died in the war, with his father dying shortly after he returns from serving at Jutland in the Navy. Suddenly, he's been left to take on this entire estate and is struggling financially,' says Tom. 'I feel that, despite his aristocratic background, he is a fairly progressive and humble man. He doesn't believe in money or land to validate himself, he doesn't feel the pressure Lord Grantham feels to carry on the legacy of his estate. But he works hard, he's got his own business and doesn't sit around expecting money to come to him. In that way, he's like Matthew – he wants to feel like he has a place in society.'

LIZ TRUBRIDGE

EXECUTIVE PRODUCER

A producer's role is often an enigmatic one, but they are, essentially, the captains steering the ship, and how they handle rough seas affects the whole crew. *Downton Abbey*, in scale and ambition, is effectively like filming nine feature movies in six months: the pressure on the production is huge and it would be understandable if there were mutinies. Fortunately, executive producer Liz Trubridge – a.k.a Queen Liz – is the oil that is poured on troubled waters. Radiating calm and good humour, with an absolute certainty in what needs to be achieved, it is Liz that navigates the good ship *Downton* the whole year round. The cast and crew are constantly amazed by her ability to keep her head when all around her chaos could break out at any moment: 'I believe in a team of equals,' she says. 'It's the way I like to work and I want everyone to feel they have a voice. As producers, our job is to pick the best team to do the job and then give them the space, facility and support to do it... because then it makes me look good!'

But her leadership is clearly inspirational. Alastair Bruce says, without hesitation, that his favourite thing about working on the show is Liz. 'She absolutely manages the team. Not only does she organise and run things, but on top of all that, she is able to make everyone feel special and brings that into her management in a way that is very comfortable to receive.'

Liz Trubridge and Brendan Patricks relax between takes.

Liz has worked on the series since its inception and is the executive producer full-time on *Downton* for the whole twelve months. Her year begins in December, when they start pre-production having received the first scripts. After the Christmas break, the pre-production process gains momentum, with more and more members of the team coming on board – department heads for design, costume and so on, then the location team, accounts team and gradually all the team members joining in. Throughout January, there are location recces, castings and meetings, and the schedule begins to come together. 'We are lucky that Julian has usually written the first four episodes by Christmas, which means we can quickly get an idea of the shape of it,' says Liz.

In February, the production is getting close to shooting and at the beginning of the month they have their 'reach recces', in which sound, camera and all crew on set (except for costume, hair and make-up) go to the locations with the directors, producers, director of photography

and line producer (who controls the budget) and checks everything out. There might, for example, be a problem with noise from the air conditioning; or the director of photography will decide he needs a lift in order to get lights for the windows; access to buildings has to be sorted; empty spaces that are going to have sets put in need to be measured up – there are countless details and factors that must be accounted for. Done properly, the crew and actors can then crack on with filming the minute they arrive.

Next is the read-through, as Liz explains: 'It's a great opportunity to hear the script for the first time and we gather as many of the cast as we possibly can. Inevitably, with the success of the show, one of the ongoing issues we have is that they are all in huge demand – we could have up to seven requests for actors' time by 10 a.m. on any given morning.' These requests could be anything from a photoshoot for a magazine cover to days needed to film scenes in a movie.

February sees the start of filming and, by then, says Liz, 'We're pleased to be up and running. We tend to start at Highclere, as it's more available in February and March, shooting in blocks of two episodes each.'

The schedule is immensely complicated. 'It's easy to forget that we are unusual in having such a huge cast,' says Liz. 'All the period costume we have to get them into – they do their make-up first, then get their clothes on, back to make-up for final tweaks. It's not uncommon to have the cast ready at 8 a.m. in 1924 hair and a beautiful costume,' she laughs.

Liz splits her time between being on set, with the directors – one will be there filming, another will be planning the next 'block' (two or three episodes) – and keeping an eye on the cutting room. The planning is detailed, as nothing can be left to chance: new actors need to be cast, directors found and the big set pieces prepared for. As viewers will have noticed, the show frequently features an elaborate event in a single episode which isn't repeated – a cricket match, a shoot, an excursion to Scotland, a garden party, Lady Rose's coming-out ball, a day at the beach – all of which need to be planned well ahead. Even if the script isn't completely finished, the producers will have been told about these beforehand.

Each block of episodes is filmed across six or so weeks, with the crew spending a third of their time at Highclere, a third at Ealing and a third at other locations, going back and forth, but as little as possible, so that the departments do not have to keep packing and moving. The final episode is filmed in late July/early August. After the wrap, pretty much everyone goes home except for Liz. 'We traditionally transmit in September [in the UK], so we deliver episodes as we film. I take a two-week break in September and come back to finish editing the final episodes. They are finished in mid-November and then off we go again, getting ready for the next series!'

The actors wait for the next scene to be set up.

DECEMBER
Christmas

CHRISTMAS

It's Christmas at Downton Abbey: the mistletoe hangs quietly, hoping to witness a kiss beneath its white berries, pine and holly are laid on every surface, a yule log crackles in the fireplace and stockings are hung on the mantelpiece.

Much of what we know and love about the festive season today was already in place by 1912, and certainly by 1924. From trees to Father Christmas and turkeys, the Victorians had largely adopted the traditions we still enjoy; Downton certainly embraces the spirit of the advent calendar.

In the great hall, a huge tree is decked out in decorations and electric lights, with piles of toys wrapped beneath – presents for the children of the estate's tenant farmers and the local village. The Countess of Warwick, at Easton Lodge, was a notorious society beauty – she was part of King Edward VII's infamous Marlborough House Set and was his lover for many years – and one of her annual traditions was a Christmas-tree party to which all the estate employees and the village schoolchildren were invited. A newspaper report described it thus: 'In the centre was a large fir-tree, taken out of the park, and reaching from the floor to the ceiling. Many hundreds of toys, of all imaginable descriptions, together with a number of sparkling brilliants, were hung upon the tree; in fact the tree was so laden that its foliage could scarcely be seen.'

At Downton Abbey, thanks to the American influence of Cora, Christmas is especially glorious. Cora would have grown up with fabulous opulence – those living in the Gilded Age, the era in which Cora was a girl in Cincinnati, made a point of putting their wealth on display at any opportunity, and Christmas was a very good opportunity indeed. The house is filled to the brim with decorations, at Cora's behest, and she may wistfully remember days of ice-skating on a lake, dressed in an elegant fur-trimmed coat.

'We've no proper
kitchen maid anymore
so we must all muck in.'
DAISY

Below stairs, the effect is not quite as astonishing, but the servants will have jollied up their quarters with some decorations, even a tree of their own in the servants' hall. For most, however, the Christmas period means an increase in their workload. Mrs Patmore will have even more cause to grumble, as she begins to plan the feast several weeks in advance. This year, of course, there are fewer servants in the kitchen than usual to help out, with Ivy having gone to work for Harold Levinson in America.

'There's a different dynamic downstairs,' says Lesley Nicol, the actress who plays Mrs Patmore. 'It's such a small unit down there that each individual contributes to the atmosphere. Now we don't have the rivalry between Ivy and Daisy anymore. Instead, Daisy's trying to develop her mind.'

Christmas Day, of course, has its roots in the Christian celebration, still keenly felt in 1924, and the morning church service would have been attended by the family and servants together. Back at the house, the family line up by the fire in the Great Hall to hand out their presents to the servants. Lord and Lady Grantham are generous and kind to their staff, so may occasionally give more than the traditional bolt of cloth for the maids to make their uniforms or stiff white collars for the footmen. In the past, Carson has received a book of the history of European royal families from Robert, while Lady Mary gave Anna a gold brooch in the shape of a heart, a token of her grateful affection.

At Downton, the servants are given luncheon off to have their own festive feast, while the family helps itself to cold cuts laid out in the dining room. This is one of only two occasions in the entire year that the Crawleys must fend for themselves (the other being drinks at midnight on New Year's Eve). Even today, says Julian Fellowes, 'The Queen has a big luncheon, fully attended, but a quiet nosh in the evening, which a small group of staff can easily manage, while they all have their beanfeast downstairs.' In the afternoon, the Crawleys amuse themselves – Mary might be persuaded to sing, while Edith plays the piano. There's an audience in the small house party staying for the week, including Rosamund, Isobel and Violet. Other guests would be encouraged to display their talents for either music or recitation. Robert will almost certainly want a walk with Isis.

'It's a Downton tradition.
They have their feast
at lunchtime
and we have ours
in the evening.'
LORD GRANTHAM

The servants will have had to save hard to buy presents, with their choice restricted to whatever is available in the shops on Ripon High Street. With their small wages, these are not grand gestures, but thoughtful items – perhaps Carson can find an umbrella for Mrs Hughes; Daisy may seek out a hat pin for Mrs Patmore. Anna and Bates are sure to spend the time thinking carefully about what the other would like and, with their occasional trips to London as lady's maid and valet, have rather more choice than the rest of their below-stairs colleagues. It seems unlikely that Thomas will go to any great effort for anyone else, but if no one else buys him even a small token, perhaps it's just as well if he ensures he has something to unwrap at the luncheon.

The servants' hall will be laid with Christmas crackers, merrily pulled to reveal the paper hats and jokes within. For once, above stairs and below enjoy more or less the same feast, from roast to plum pudding. Frederick Gorst, butler at Carden Park after the First World War, recalled a sumptuous repast for the servants: 'Four long tables and wooden benches had been set up for the dinner, which was served at one o'clock. First a great hog's head, stuffed with sausage meat and pate de foie gras from the Squire's own geese, was carried in by four men and set upon a separate table. It had a shiny red apple in its mouth and the ferns and greens which decorated the huge board lent a pagan touch. Then came the cold meats and roasts. The main dish consisted of the finest joints of beef and Yorkshire pudding and many kinds of vegetables. And finally the plum pudding was brought in, burning and flaming with brandy.'

Mrs Patmore is a powerful figure at Christmas, when so much of the attention is focused on the foodstuffs. The truth is, the cooks were pretty powerful most of the time. They ran their own dominion in the kitchen. Mrs Patmore may have to ask Carson if she wants time off, but the kitchen maids are hers to boss as she wishes. Cooks were set apart by the fact that although they were servants, they did not directly serve the family; aside from her weekly meetings with Cora to decide the menu, Mrs Patmore would have very little to do with anyone beyond the green baize door. Combine that with many long hours in a steamy basement room and the daily tick-tock pressure to send out delicious dishes on time, and it's not hard to see why their blood pressure often reached the same boiling point as the kettle. Good cooks who bore the conditions were treasured by the families that employed them and any foibles were considered the price you paid for delicious food on your table.

For Christmas Day, Mrs Patmore will have her kitchen staff make as much as they possibly can, but it is a time for luxurious indulgence too. Hampers will have been ordered from London's Fortnum & Mason and Harrods. The larder will be full of game from the estate's shoots. There's a plentiful supply of vegetables, meat and dairy from the home farm too. In 1924, more and more foods are being imported from abroad, bringing exotic delights to the dining table via the bigger stores, and even one or two ambitious York suppliers.

But even with all this at her fingertips, Mrs Patmore is driven to work as hard as she ever did – she needs to prove to her employers that she is indispensable. Talk of refrigerators frightens her and the introduction into the kitchen of electric beaters and toasters will not prevent an old-fashioned cook like Mrs P. from making absolutely every element of the Christmas feast from scratch, from quince jelly to brandy butter.

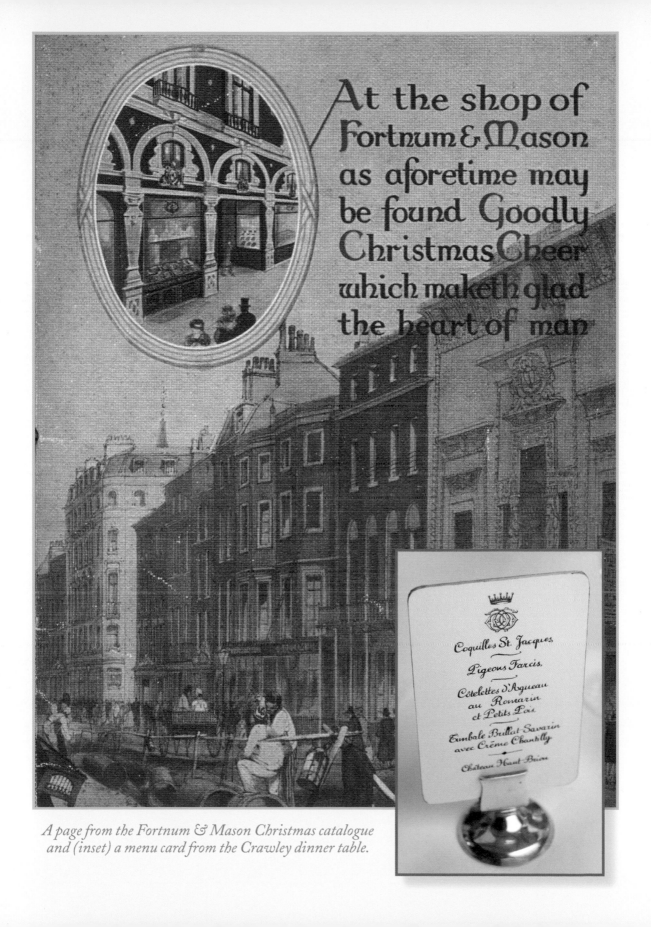

At the shop of Fortnum & Mason as aforetime may be found Goodly Christmas Cheer which maketh glad the heart of man

Coquilles St. Jacques,

Pigeons Farcis,

Côtelettes d'Agneau au Romarin et Petits Pois,

Timbale Brillat-Savarin avec Crème Chantilly

Château Haut-Brion

A page from the Fortnum & Mason Christmas catalogue and (inset) a menu card from the Crawley dinner table.

CHRISTMAS PUDDING

No Christmas at Downton Abbey would be complete without plum pudding, as it is also known (somewhat confusingly, it does not contain any plums — this was a pre-Victorian word for raisins). The pudding should be prepared up to three months in advance and kept in a cool, dark place.

MAKES 1 LARGE PUDDING TO SERVE 8–10

100g white breadcrumbs
50g self-raising flour
100g chopped suet
1 tsp mixed spice
¼ tsp ground nutmeg
¼ tsp ground cinnamon
225g soft dark brown sugar
250g raisins
250g sultanas
25g mixed peel or finely
   chopped dried apricots
1 small apple, coarsely grated
25g flaked almonds
zest of 1 lemon
zest of 1 orange
2 eggs
150ml Guinness or stout
2 tablespoons brandy
   (plus extra for setting
   the pudding aflame)
butter, for greasing

Place all the dry ingredients, fruit, almonds and citrus zest in a large mixing bowl and stir well. Combine the eggs, Guinness and 2 tablespoons of the brandy in a jug and whisk together, then pour into the bowl and fold in until well combined — it should now have a dropping consistency, but add a little more stout if necessary. Cover and leave overnight to allow the flavours to mingle and the mixture to thicken.

Next day, butter a 1.2 litre pudding basin. Use the basin to trace and cut out two circles of greaseproof paper — one the size of the bottom and one the size of the top. Line the bottom of the basin with the small circle of paper. Fill the basin with the mixture to about 1cm from the top and pat down with a wooden spoon. Cover the pudding with the larger circle of greaseproof paper, so it is sitting on the mixture. Lay a sheet of foil over the top, doming it slightly to allow the pudding to swell. Tie a piece of string around the basin, under the rim, to secure the foil in place.

Place a metal pastry cutter or muffin ring in the base of a large pan, and set the pudding on the ring in the bottom of the pan (this ensures the basin does not crack). If the basin is a tight fit in the pan you can tie an additional loop of string over the top of the pudding, to help you lift it out of the pan later. Add boiling water to come halfway up the side of the basin. Cover the pan with a lid and simmer steadily for 8 hours, adding more boiling water from time to time, as needed.

Wearing oven gloves, carefully remove the basin from the pan and leave it to cool.

When the pudding is cold, wrap in foil and store in a cool, dark place.

Before serving, the pudding should be steamed once again for 2 hours. On Christmas Day, turn it out on to a flat dish and stick a sprig of holly in the centre. Warm a ladleful of brandy, pour it over the pudding and set light to it just before you carry it to the table.

BRANDY BUTTER

This is a popular accompaniment to Christmas pudding and is known as 'hard sauce' in the US. It can be made several days in advance, as it keeps very well.

SERVES 8–10

200g unsalted butter,
    softened
175g icing sugar
1 teaspoon vanilla extract
6 tablespoons brandy

Place the butter in a mixing bowl and beat with an electric hand whisk until pale and smooth. Add the icing sugar and vanilla extract, and beat until it is all incorporated. Add the brandy gradually, to taste, and stir well.

Spoon the brandy butter into a small serving dish, cover and store in the fridge until needed. Serve very cold, with the Christmas pudding.

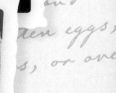

Cover each pud... slightly to all... string around ... handle across the top; ... ...in and out of the pan.

Despite all the changes in the kitchen, one thing has resolutely stayed the same. 'Her work ethic,' says Lesley of her character. 'It's not changed and it never will. She's proud of her job and has high standards.' At Christmas, when it's more important than ever to put on a good show, Mrs Patmore will be pulling all the rabbits out of the hat (and into the cooking pot).

Service is Mrs P.'s world; she's barely out of the kitchen, let alone Downton village. 'It's the disappearance of the structure she knows,' says Lesley. 'We've got to know more about her insecurities. She started as a slightly scary woman, indomitable and hard-faced, but Julian's allowed us to see her frailties and her more vulnerable side, which of course everybody has. We've stripped away the professional layers to reveal the woman beneath.

'I do think she's happy. We have to bear in mind the time – in those days people were less concerned with their own happiness. Instead they thought about their sense of duty, belonging, respect – all of those things make her content in that she has achieved something. She has security: a good position, a roof over her head, a chum in Mrs Hughes, she's fond of Daisy and people even laugh at her jokes!'

'Daisy? What's happened to you? I said you could go for a drink of water, not a trip up the Nile!'

MRS PATMORE

Ah, yes, the quick remarks. Mrs Patmore is the below-stairs version of Violet: they are both the matriarchs of their domains, set in their ways – resistant, even frightened, of change – but unbowed when it comes to protecting their family. And they both have the same wry wit. 'Julian said at a press conference in New York that he didn't originally write Mrs P. as a funny character, suggesting that I had brought something to it as an actor,' reveals Lesley. Nor was this the only way in which her portrayal may have affected Julian's scripts. 'I think because I get on so well with Sophie [McShera] and we love working together, there's a real chemistry. I think he saw that and took the potential to investigate it. There's more of a mother and daughter dynamic between her and Daisy now.'

Isobel
Crawley

When the servants have finished their luncheon, the footmen serve tea in the library and the family give their presents. To each other, they will be naturally indulgent, although nothing like on the scale that is frequently seen today. Mary and Edith may have done their shopping in London, bringing back glass bottles of scent, fine silk stockings, small items of jewellery and leather-bound books. Robert probably best appreciates a box of cigars. Violet may have had to do with finding her presents in the village, though one rather imagines her to be the type to re-wrap something she was given before that she didn't like and pass it along. There's always room, too, for the hidden message: Isobel has given her a nutcracker.

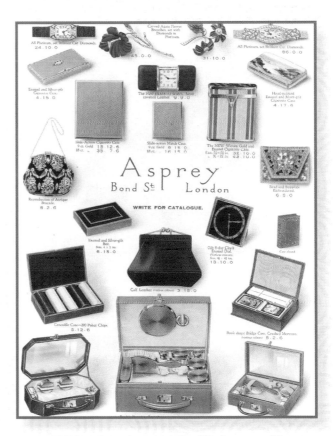

1920s advertisement for Christmas gifts from Asprey, Bond Street.

CHARADES

In the drawing room, the fire is blazing and games are played. The favourite of the Crawleys is The Game, which was played by British families all over the land (nowadays it is more usually called Charades). Julian took the idea from his own childhood Christmases. One side gives a player in the opposing team a title – a book, song or opera – which they must then mime to their own team. Absolutely no speaking is allowed by the actor, though the guessers are usually increasingly shrill as they fail to get it correctly.

Charades, as played by the Victorians, was quite different – it took much more time to set up and play, which was why The Game took over in popularity. A phrase or word would be chosen by a team and broken up into smaller parts, each of which would be elaborately acted out using costumes and props. The opposing side would have to guess the phrase. So, for example, 'Downton Abbey' might consist of a scene of people pretending to ski down a hill; then acting out 'the ton' (the nickname for members of high society in the Regency era); finally, monks praying in an abbey.

An alternative, rather funny game, is In the Manner of the Word. One person leaves the room and everyone else decides on an adjective – slowly, quickly, stupidly, angrily; the person returns and asks individuals to act something out 'in the manner of the word'. So a player will comb their hair excitedly, or pretend to paint a picture idiotically, or whatever. Whomever acts out the word successfully enough for the guesser to get it right is the next one out of the room.

'Life is a game, in which the player must appear ridiculous.'

VIOLET, DOWAGER
COUNTESS OF GRANTHAM

At 6 p.m., as usual, the dressing gong sounds and everyone dresses for dinner. Although things have become more relaxed in 1924, at Christmas, it will be white tie, just as it has been for over a century at Downton Abbey. There may be a fairly large party for dinner, with outer branches of the Crawley family tree present, as well as some of the grander local families. Champagne is drunk and the star of the show will undoubtedly be Mrs Patmore's pudding, with a sprig of holly on top and flaming brandy. Violet plunges in the first spoon, wishing one and all a happy Christmas as she does so.

Grand houses, or certainly those with at least twenty servants, such as Downton Abbey, would hold a servants' ball, usually in the days between Christmas and New Year, though there were no hard and fast rules about this. King Edward VII, at Sandringham, annually held three balls on a single night: the county ball for the local elite, the tenants' ball for the leading families of the shire and one for the servants.

The ball would be attended, obviously, by all the servants of the house, and sometimes those from other smaller, local houses would be invited too. The party would start when the master of the house had the first dance with the housekeeper, and the mistress with the butler. Eileen Balderson, a maid of that time, recalled her sister making a faux pas at a house where she was head kitchen maid. The eldest son of the family asked her for the first dance and, not knowing who he was, she said she was already promised to someone else: 'The mistake is readily explained. Except for the butler's pantry staff and the lady's maid, the rest of the servants very rarely saw the family, the kitchen staff least of all.'

Thankfully for the servants, the family would leave after half an hour, at which point a servants' ball could become livelier. Especially once the butler, cook and their guests had left. 'After that it was really enjoyable!' remembers Eileen. Servants' balls usually only began at 10 p.m., so they would find themselves out of their beds for the whole night, with just a quick wash and change of clothes before returning to work in the morning. And so on, for another year…

FURTHER READING

The Green Hat, (a novel), Michael Arlen, W. Collins Sons & Co. Ltd, 1924

The Last Country Houses, Clive Aslet, Book Club Associates, 1982

Backstairs Life in a Country House, Eileen Balderson, David & Charles, 1982

The Glitter and the Gold, Consuelo Vanderbilt Balsan, George Mann, 1973

Hutch, Charlotte Breese, Bloomsbury, 1999

Etiquette of Good Society, Lady Colin Campbell, Cassell & Company, 1893

The Decline & Fall of the British Aristocracy, David Cannadine, Picador, 1990

Christmas with the Savages, Mary Clive, Jane Nissen Books, 2008

The Rainbow Comes and Goes, Diana Cooper, Penguin, 1958

Life in the English Country House, Mark Girouard, Yale University Press, 1978

The Lady's Maid, Rosina Harrison, Ebury Press, 1975

The Perfect Hostess, Rose Henniker Heaton, Methuen & Co., 1931

1920s Fashion Design, edited by Joost Hölscher, Pepin Press, 1998

Life Below Stairs in the Twentieth Century, Pamela Horn, Amberley, 2010

The Green Baize Door, Ernest King, as told to Richard Viner, William Kimber, 1963

Women's Dress in the Jazz Age, James Laver, Hamish Hamilton, 1964

Servants: A Downstairs View of Twentieth-century Britain, Lucy Lethbridge, Bloomsbury, 2013

Gentlemen Prefer Blondes, (a novel), Anita Loos, Picador, 1925

To Marry An English Lord, Gail MacColl and Carol McD. Wallace, Workman Publishing, 1989

Up and Down Stairs: The History of the Country House Servant, Jeremy Musson, John Murray, 2010

Singled Out: How Two Million Women Survived Without Men after the First World War, Virginia Nicholson, Penguin, 2008

How To Be Asked Again: How To Be The Perfect Shooting Guest, Rosie Nickerson, Quiller Press, 2009

The Great Silence: 1918–1920 Living in the Shadow of the Great War, Juliet Nicolson, John Murray, 2009

The Duff Cooper Diaries, edited by John Julius Norwich, Phoenix, 2006

The Bolter, Frances Osborne, Virago Press, 2008

The Perfect Debutante, Adrian Porter, Collins, 1937

Below Stairs, Margaret Powell, Pan Books, 1968

Bluestockings: The Remarkable Story of the First Women to Fight for an Education, Jane Robinson, Penguin, 2010

This Was My World, Viscountess Rhondda, Macmillan & Co., 1933

Modern Britain: A Social History 1750–1997, Edward Royle, Hodder Education, 1997

The Big Shots: Edwardian Shooting Parties, Jonathan Ruffer, Quiller Press, 1977

The Clear Stream: A Life of Winifred Holtby, Marion Shaw, Virago, 2000

A Nice Clean Plate: Recollections 1919–1931, Lavinia Smiley, Michael Russell (Publishing) Ltd, 1981

Wise Parenthood, Marie Carmichael Stopes, G.P. Putnam's Sons, Ltd, 1918

Tea By The Nursery Fire, Noel Streatfeild, Virago, an imprint of Little, Brown Book Group, 1975

Farmer's Glory, A.G. Street, Faber Finds, 2011

Bright Young People, D. J. Taylor, Random House, 2007

The Book of Etiquette, Lady Troubridge, The Kingswood Press, 1926

What The Butler Saw, E. S. Turner, Penguin,1962

The Unexpurgated Beaton Diaries, introduced by Hugo Vickers, Phoenix, 2003

Life's Ebb and Flow, Frances.Countess of Warwick, William Morrow & Company, 1929

The Country House Remembered, edited by Merlin Waterson, Routledge, Kegan & Paul, 1985

Grace and Favour: Memoirs of Loelia Duchess of Westminster, Weidenfeld & Nicolson, 1961

COOKERY

Modern Cookery for Private Families, Eliza Acton, Quadrille, 2011 (first published 1845)

Mrs Beeton's Book of Household Management, Isabella Beeton, Ward, Lock & Co., 1911 (first published 1861)

Mrs Beeton's Cold Sweets, Isabella Beeton, Ward, Lock & Co., 1925

Mrs Beeton's Hors d'Oeuvres and Savouries, Isabella Beeton, Ward, Lock & Co., 1925

Mrs Beeton How to Cook, Isabella Beeton and Gerard Baker, Weidenfeld & Nicolson, 2011

Simple French Cooking for English Homes, Xavier Marcel Boulestin, Quadrille, 2011 (first published 1923)

Arabella Boxer's Book of English Food, Fig Tree, 2012

Margaret Costa's Four Seasons Cookery Book, Thomas Nelson & Sons Ltd, 1970

The Oxford Companion to Food, Alan Davidson, Oxford University Press, 1999

A History of English Food, Clarissa Dickson Wright, Random House Books, 2011

Jane Grigson's English Food, Ebury Press, 1992, (first published 1974)

Food in England, Dorothy Hartley, Piatkus, 2009

The Gentle Art of Cookery, Miss Olga Hartley and Mrs C. F. Leyel, Quadrille, 2011 (first published 1925)

The Pauper's Cookbook, Jocasta Innes, Penguin Books Ltd, 1971

Larousse Gastronomique, Prosper Montagné, Paul Hamlyn Ltd, 1961

The Downstairs Cookbook, Margaret Powell, Macmillan, 2012

Good Things in England, Florence White, Persephone Books, 1999 (first published 1932)

RECIPE INDEX

PICTURE CREDITS

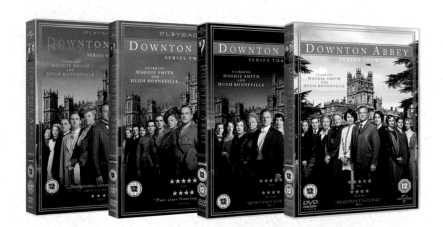

Indulge yourself with another visit to DOWNTON ABBEY on DVD and Blu-ray

ACKNOWLEDGEMENTS

To have been given the opportunity to write my third companion book to *Downton Abbey* has been a privilege. Delving back into the extraordinary world created by Julian Fellowes, Gareth Neame and the exceptionally talented cast and crew is, as any fan may imagine, nothing less than sheer delight. That they allow me to do so with patience and grace on their side, excitement and idiot questions on mine, is luck indeed.

I've had the good fortune to work with Headline Publishing Group for this book and my gratitude to them for their hard work and encouragement is deep – especially to Sarah Emsley, Yeti Lambregts and Holly Harris. Also to Frances Gough and Vicky Palmer in publicity and marketing. Project manager Jenny Wheatley kept me on course, Juliana Foster's intelligent edits prevented me from making an ass of myself (and if she missed anything, *mea culpa*) and designer Pene Parker has made the words look a thing of beauty. Of course, we would be nothing without the beautiful photography of Nick Briggs – thank you, Nick.

I'm also very excited that St Martin's Press are publishing this edition in the US – what a pleasure to work again with executive editor Hope Dellon, publicist John Karle and Silissa Kenney.

My thanks go to my agent, Caroline Michel, and her assistant, Christine Okoth at Peters, Fraser & Dunlop. Also to Annabel Murello for making it all happen in the first place.

Major thanks to Jessica Morris of Milk Publicity who had the hideous task of setting up the interviews between the cast, crew and me during filming – in other words, when everyone had about as much spare time between takes as Father Christmas on Christmas Eve.

To authors past and present I give thanks for their knowledge, truthfulness and gravitas – I hope readers of this book will take the inspiration I did from the Further Reading list. I was also fortunate enough to receive expert advice from Hunters law firm on the intricacies of 1920s family law. This book would be full of terrible errors were it not for the insight and eagle eye of Emma Kitchener-Fellowes. Thank you, Emma, for so much more than just the book.

Finally, the biggest thank you goes to my family, who endure my absence, distraction and bad suppers as I hurry to my deadline. I couldn't do it without you and I'm so glad you are all here: Simon, Beatrix, Louis and George.

Downton Abbey
A Carnival Films/Masterpiece Co-production

First published in Great Britain in 2014
by HEADLINE PUBLISHING GROUP

1

Cataloguing in Publication Data is available from the British Library

Hardback ISBN 978 1 4722 2053 0

Photography by Nick Briggs
Additional photography by Noel Murphy and Nick Wall (see picture credits on page 318)
Design by Pene Parker

Typeset in Caslon and Futura
Printed and bound in Germany by Mohn Media

HEADLINE PUBLISHING GROUP
An Hachette UK Company
338 Euston Road
London NW1 3BH
www.headline.co.uk
www.hachette.co.uk